THE PEAK

'Things are as they are because they were as they were.'

THOMAS GOLD, ASTRONOMER

THE PEAK

Past and present

GORDON STAINFORTH

CONSTABLE
LONDON

FIRST PUBLISHED IN GREAT BRITAIN 1998
BY CONSTABLE AND COMPANY LIMITED
3 THE LANCHESTERS, 162 FULHAM PALACE ROAD
LONDON W6 9ER

DESIGNED, AND SET IN ADOBE GARAMOND, BY THE AUTHOR
PRINTED IN HONG KONG THROUGH WORLD PRINT LTD

A CIP CATALOGUE RECORD FOR THIS BOOK IS AVAILABLE FROM

Geoff Douglas on the classic
'Moyer's Buttress' on Gardom's
Edge

◄ Climbing the Baldstone
Arête in the heart of the area
known to the Celts as Anu's
Rocks (Ann Roach). The
Baldstone is the Stone of the
Norse Sun God, Balder

Climber: Steve Dean

CONTENTS

1 Rock and stars

We have no means of knowing whether Neolithic man ever had the time or the inclination to climb on the rocks around his caves at Harboro ('boundary stronghold'); probably his day-to-day preoccupation with the 'chase' was more than adequate sport. Surrounded by prowling bears and sabre-toothed tigers, wolves and hyena, bison and lemmings, he surely had other things on his mind than the mundaneness of the rock.

But to make such an assumption is to misunderstand his appreciation of this most fundamental of all substances. For practically everything on which his survival depended – his tools, weapons and shelters – had to be made of it, and his whole life was thus totally bound up with it. While it would perhaps be an exaggeration to say that he loved it, his relationship with it was necessarily an intimate one. He understood every nuance of it, in all its varieties: how gritstone could be split, chert sharpened and limestone polished.

But his involvement with the rock extended beyond the merely practical; there was undoubtedly a spiritual dimension too. These rocky hilltops were not just the home of the dead; they were also mysteriously linked with the starry heavens above. Underpinning all his beliefs was his deep conviction that 'as above, so below' – that the whole cycle of life was somehow regulated by the life and movement of the stars. Every rocky tor and hilltop nearest the stars, such as Aleck Low, Minninglow and Harboro, was a sacred site, each having the dual function of burial ground and place of worship.

◀ Climbing at Harboro at the Spring Equinox

▶ Harboro on an October evening

◀ The 'Winking Man', Ramshaw Rocks, which overlooked an ancient trackway, and later, a Roman road

OUT OF THE STARS

It was not just that spirits dwelt in these rocky hilltops but that the rock itself had certain magical properties. The 'Wishing Stone' in Lumsdale was already well known for making dreams come true if you walked around it three times, and stones with natural holes through them, such as a famous one on the nearby Holestone Moor, were regarded as having both sexual and healing powers. If the hole was big enough, a whole baby would be passed through it to protect it from illness, or a couple would clasp hands through it to ensure their prolonged fertility.

But the magic went further than this; the ancient People of the Peak had the dim but certain intuition, four millennia before scientists could confirm it, that the mysterious substance of this carboniferous rock had a special relationship to *us* – and that rock, man and stars were here part of some gigantic cosmic equation, one great energy system. But it was not until 1913 that the Harvard scientist Lawrence Henderson was able to say quite categorically – once it was known that the element carbon (the source of all life) had *come from* the stars – that the universe was in its very essence 'biocentric'. Astrophysical research has since shown that stars are enormous nuclear furnaces producing carbon from helium by a complicated process which the astronomer Fred Hoyle famously described as looking like a 'put-up job' – as if the laws of nuclear physics were 'deliberately designed with regard to the consequences they produce inside the stars'. Very recently another cosmologist, Paul Davies, has said that we may regard ourselves, in a perfectly scientific sense, as 'children of the universe – animated stardust'. Which seems to me to be exactly the way the Bronze Age People of the Peak saw themselves.

Nor perhaps would they have been particularly surprised to learn that this carboniferous limestone had once been made up of living creatures and that in due course, broken down by water or fire, it would become carbon dioxide, the essential molecule for the growth of all plant life.

▶ Seven minute exposure of Cassiopeia and the circumpolar stars over Rainster Rocks in early May

◄ Nine Ladies Stone Circle,
Stanton Moor

COSMIC MARRIAGE PROBLEMS

These People of the Heights knew that by erecting stones in a circle, so that they aligned with crucial transits of the sun and moon, their powers could be channelled. Far more than just arcane astronomical computers, they were, in the archaeologist John Barnatt's phrase, 'temples of integration and harmony', a natural focal point and sacred centre for an entire community. But what has also emerged from recent studies is that the stone circles of the Peak District reflect an all-abiding fascination, described by Barnatt as an obsession, with the basic numbers 1 to 10 – the Decad.

In particular, the numbers 3, 7 and 9 fascinated them because of the way they related to the mysteries of the moon-goddess. Unlike Lu, the two-faced sun-god of summer and winter, Anu, the moon-goddess – who waxed, became full, and waned each month – was triple-aspected, being the goddess of life, procreation and death. And she had two daughters who were also triple-aspected: the gentle and benign Ellen and the tough and cruel Brigantia (the warrior-goddess of the Brigantes). Each represented maiden, bride and mother: virginity, fertility, and maternity. Always looking into past, present and future. A triad of triple-aspected goddesses, an ennead – the balanced perfection of the triangle now enlarged into the closed and never-ending perfection of the circle.

But there was one great problem, a fundamental disharmony at the root of all existence and the probable cause of all strife in the world, which baffled them; and that was the apparent incompatibility of the sun and the moon, Lu and Anu. Lu, all-powerful, but only for a season, was of absolutely no importance without Anu, who was the earth mother and the source of all fertility. Yet their activities seemed completely unrelated. Anu's menstrual cycle of 28 days, which was crucial to all fertility, did not coincide in any obvious way with Lu's annual transit which governed the seasons. Worse, their apparent total independence frustrated all attempts at establishing a simple working calendar. Odd days had to be added to make the months fit the year, and it was the exception rather than the rule for any of the four sun festivals (of the solstices and the equinoxes) to coincide with the full moon.

Sunset from Win Hill

And then they made an interesting discovery: they found after long observation that roughly every eighteen years, sometimes nineteen, the full moon would coincide once more with the midsummer solstice, and the whole complicated cycle would start again. For nine years the moon would rise further and further north on the eastern horizon, and then for another nine years it would retreat southwards again.

Two important stone circles in the Peak – each with nine stones – reflect these findings: the ingenious Nine Stones on Harthill Moor, marking all the important transits of the sun and moon, and the Nine Ladies Circle on Stanton Moor, which has an extra outlying stone, probably representing Brigantia, or even Anu herself.

THE GREEN MAN OF THE DERWENT

The ancient woodland below
Gardom's Edge in November

Newcomers from central Europe arrived in the Peak in about 500 BC, bringing with
them the invention of iron and, it seems, worsening weather; indeed, that was why the
Celts came: to escape the harsh, icebound winters of the Continent. In these colder,
stormier times they descended into the densely forested sanctuary of the Derwent and
its tributaries, making clearings with their new iron axes. Here, surrounded by wild
boar, red deer, and pigs gorging themselves on acorns, they found a complete support
system of water, firewood and food.

With this new environment came a whole new culture which centred on the oak
tree. The very name of the valley, *Derwent*, was Celtic for 'thick with oaks', while the
name of the wise men who guarded this culture, the druids (*derwyddon*), meant 'knowers
of the oak'. Much more than just priests, they combined the roles of astronomer, prophet,
healer, magician, ritual curser (of enemies) and supervisor of sacrifices (some apparently
human). The Stone Age idea of life residing in and deriving from the rock and the stars
had expanded into a multifaceted and immensely subtle system that embraced the
whole of nature. The mother-goddess of the earth was now aided by her daughters, the
spring- and water- goddesses, with the tree-god acting as a sort of mediator. Rivers and
springs became the most important of all natural features, as is reflected by the fact that
all the rivers of the Peak have Celtic names.

More than just the sources of drinking-water and irrigation, springs were recognized, like the rocks of old, as having special curative and regenerative powers. Accordingly, they became the sanctuaries of Anu – for example, Anu's Nemeton (or sacred grove) at the source of the Wye at Buxton – or of her daughter, the local water-sprite Elian, with wells at Wirksworth, Darley and Eyam. Such places as the Ebbing and Flowing Well in Barmoor Clough were womb openings of the earth mother, the source of all life, which ebbs and flows according to the moon.

Equally important was Hob, the guardian spirit of the woods. He was none other than the old horned god of the Bronze Age, now reappearing with a suitably green complexion. As the horned god he was 'Lord of All the Stags' – indeed, of all the animals; as Herne the Hunter he was god of the chase. In his in-between state he was the *horned huntsman* – the Green Man – the hunter and the hunted become one.

The 'Black Stream' (the Dove) and Thorpe Cloud in a hard winter

◄ Between rock and sky: a rowan tree grows out of the magnesium limestone of Roystone Rocks near Minninglow

▼ Rowan berries in Alport Dale in November

ALL ONE LIFE

With no sharp division between the natural and the supernatural, the spiritual and the physical, the sky and the earth, the whole landscape, indeed the whole cosmos, was regarded as magic through and through, and filled with the spirits of people and gods. Everything was interrelated. All the gods and forces of nature, all the spirits of the living and the dead, shared One Life; and every living thing had a soul which would transmigrate and live again for ever in different forms. Heroic hunter-warriors, for example, would become one with Hob, who in turn could assume many guises, be it stag or roebuck, giant, wood elf or Green Man.

A tree: an intermediary between rock and sky – life itself coming out of the mother earth. For ever earthbound, but nevertheless drawing some of its power from the sky. The rowan in particular was regarded as having magical properties, so that it was only natural that when the People of the Plateau started to extract lead from the limestone, they planted rowans at the entrance of their mines in the belief that this would encourage the lead ore to *grow*.

Dead rowan tree at the site of the ancient fort at Aldwark

There was a particularly strong superstition about cutting down old trees, especially yews and long-dead oaks. In addition to rocks and monoliths, they were the embodiment of the spirits of dead ancestors. The yew, which lived even longer than the oak, was the most venerated of all trees. In a typically paradoxical way, the Celts regarded this tree, which seemed to live for ever – the famous Darley yew, for example, is said to be nearly 2,000 years old – as the 'death tree', which would 'spread a root to the mouth of each corpse' in a graveyard. As Hamlet's uncle later knew, the juice from its berry was lethal if poured into the ear, and yet it was the best-known antidote for the bite of a viper.

Because the soul transmigrated and lived on in nature, the Celts saw death not as the end of life but as the midpoint in a continuous life. While some gods still lived underground (Hob, for example, lived in caves and tumuli, like Hob's House in Monsal Dale and Hob's Hurst House near Chatsworth), they had no notion of a hellish underworld of the dead, having already replaced burials with cremation. Rather, they believed in an *Otherworld*, another dimension which pervaded the whole living cosmos. Far from seeing it as a realm of death, they actually called it the 'Land of the Living', which the dead return to and the living come out of.

IN BETWEEN

The Celts had a supremely balanced view of the world which enabled them to appreciate the whole cycle of nature in all its richness. The contending forces of fertility and virility, yin and yang, female and male (and, indeed, women and men's roles in the community) were seen as interdependent, as different sides, as it were, of one coin. Each season was vital in its own way. Everything had not just an opposite but an all-important intermediate aspect, just as life itself was an in-between state. At the borders, at which everything hung in the balance – between light and darkness, summer and winter, life and death (or, rather, rebirth) – lay the key to existence. Not for the Celts a simplistic world of polarities or confrontational dualities, but something altogether more subtle; a world of balanced triplicities – of triangles and nine-pointed circles rather than squares.

Theirs was also a very optimistic view of life, with everything seen always in the most positive light: the in-between state of the beginning of winter was the *start* of a new year, the brief period each month when there was no moon was the *new* moon, and the twilight zone after the sun had set was the *start* of a new day.

The Celtic world-view is beautifully summarized in the metaphor of the harp that can play three airs: the grief strain, the sleep strain and the laughter strain, sleep being the dream state between life and death – the tragicomic fantasy in which much of life is and should be lived.

▶ All one life: Ramshaw Rocks and Rosebay Willowherb below Plum Buttress, Chee Dale, in October

… a gross succession of ghoulish faces, bovine and porcine heads, and half-finished monsters springing from the parent rock.

Ernest Baker

Bamford Edge at the Autumn equinox

Midsummer sunset from Nine Stones

MIDSUMMER MOON DANCE

It is the evening of a Sun Day: the start of the Full Moon Day at the summer solstice, AD 42. And, as is happening at several stone circles in the Peak today, the people of Harthill Moor are gathering at Nine Stones for an unusually important moon dance. For this year – as happens only every eighteen years – the midsummer full moon reaches its lowest transit in the night sky. Today, after a perfect consummation with Lu a fortnight ago, Brigantia, the High One, will attain her greatest powers.

Just before sunset the great fire at the centre of the Nine Stones is lit, and the large wicker cage holding Tup, the ram of sacrifice, is lowered slowly on to the pyre. Then, as the fiery sun goes down in the north-west, golden and exhausted, so in perfect balance up soars the great disc of Anu in all her pregnancy from behind the woods of the south-east skyline.

For a while there is no sound, and then, as the first flames reach the wicker basket, Tup begins to squeal and everyone starts to chant in unison, throwing dead oak branches on to the fire. As the heat of the fire increases, they all start to discard their clothing, and a solitary piper begins his strange bird-like music. Before long, they are 'clipping' – holding hands in an unbroken chain and dancing widdershins, anti-sunwise, in a wild circle around the outside of the great stones. The pace becomes ever faster, the wild cries ever more ecstatic, as they are possessed by the virility of the stones and the sexuality of Anu. In the dense smoke and orange light of the flames, they enter a collective dream state in which the divine and the animal in man become one, and past, present and future merge in one orgiastic moment of pure joy.

All the time the fulsome disc of the moon-goddess is making its serene and relentless way across the southern sky …

▶ Moonrise over Thorpe Cloud

HOB'S STRIDE

It is long after midnight, and the moon dance is over. Most of the people have long since retired to the warmer confines of the roundhut to continue their procreational activities out of sight of the elders. But why are these elders still standing in a little huddle by the remains of the fire and staring, transfixed, at the familiar outcrop of Hob's Hall, silhouetted against the night sky? Why is the Chief Druid looking so worried?

The truth is that the great climax of the festival – for the stargazers, at least – has only just begun. The great orb of the moon has just touched the left-hand 'horn' or turret of Hob's Hall, and all have fallen silent, following intently the exact line of its transit, on which so much depends. It passes completely below the top of the left horn, and then begins to skim along the central ridge-crest.

Hob himself is watching on the crest between the horns, his antlers clearly visible against the brightness of the moon as he bestrides this great symbol of the cult animal of the Peak. Then, as the moon reaches the right-hand pinnacle, there are loud and alarmed mutterings. All is far from well; the prophets of doom have been proved right. The exact line that Anu has taken tonight – at what is already the lowest point in the eighteen-year cycle – is even lower than usual, the lowest, indeed, that anyone can ever remember seeing it. And that can mean only one thing: there will certainly be an eclipse of the sun within the next few weeks.

The Celts may have had a reputation for fearlessness, but now the elders are full of

The moon reaches the right-hand pinnacle of Hob's Hall

fear. What they are perhaps most afraid of is their own ignorance. They are going to have to warn the people, so that they are not unduly alarmed when the awful darkening occurs; but what on mother's earth are they going to say when they are asked to explain what it *means*?

The more they have studied and learned about the movements of the stars (and the Wanderers in particular), the more acutely they appreciate just how little they truly understand the workings of the heavens and the earth. Whenever there is some strange and terrible portent, like an eclipse or a comet – when the gods are clearly sending them a message – it seldom relates in any obvious way with subsequent events. Indeed, sometimes these signs have actually brought them *good* luck, while some of the worst disasters, like plagues or bad harvests, have come without any warning at all.

All they can do now is brace themselves for the worst and hope for the best.

Comet Hale-Bopp over Minninglow

2 Damnati in metalla

TRESPASSERS

The first of the bad tidings came the very next year, in AD 43. The sound of horses' hooves in the distance – the harbinger of doom, a lone messenger on horseback, coming at a gallop up the Old Portway, the track that ran past Nine Stones Close. Very bad news: a vast army from far away across the seas, known as the Romani, had landed in Britain and was sweeping all before it.

For the next four years there were tales of nothing but carnage. And then, in AD 47, the worst: these empire-building wreckers, who boastfully styled themselves 'the Unconquered', had overrun the Coritani and were even now ranged all along their southern border river (which they called 'the Trespasser', the Trent, on account of the frequency with which it burst its banks). But that was not all. Disbelieving, uncomprehending, they heard that their young warrior-queen, Cartimandua, had charmed the Roman commander and done some kind of *peace deal*. Apparently, they were now an 'independent client kingdom' – whatever that meant – and a 'frontier zone' had been agreed on, with forts on *both* sides of the Trespasser.

The druids were furious. 'Do not trust them. They rob, kill and rape and call it "civilization"; they drive people from their homes and call it peace.' And so it happened: an enormous wooden fort was built on the west bank of the Derwent just south of Dove Field, and the locals who tried to oppose it were all rounded up and executed.

After this atrocity there was, for a time, an uneasy peace. It seemed that these 'Mediterranean' invaders, who were continually moaning about the British weather, were wary of the dangers that lurked in the caves and forests of the Peak. It was already well known that they were a profoundly unspiritual and morbidly superstitious people: they were clearly terrified of Hob's Houses (his burial mounds and his caves), not to mention the stone circles and sacrificial altars. The theory even got about that they were not really interested in Brigantea.

No! insisted the druids; they're up to something.

And sure enough, before very long, Roman prospectors – apparently sanctioned by Cartimandua – were wandering quite openly into the Low Peak around Harboro. Trespassing, prying, trying to extract information about the lead mines, and soon paying large sums of money to any miner who would extract the lead for them. Almost overnight, it seemed, the stability of life on the limestone plateau had collapsed, with the subcontractors *(conductores)* working for the Romans becoming very rich and having the cheek to call themselves 'The Society of the Hammerers of Lu' (*Socii Lutudarenses*), and acrimonious disputes breaking out as to who exactly owned which mining areas. The druids were appalled by the new, Roman concept of *commercium* – the idea that these sacred rocks could be smashed up and used for commercial gain.

◄ Minninglow from Roystone Rocks

WARRIOR-QUEEN TURNS TRAITOR

Meanwhile, the Twentieth Legion had been busy in the far west (in what is now central Wales) crushing the bellicose Ordovices. When they were finally defeated in AD 51, their guerilla leader, Caratacus, fled to the Brigantes for safety. But Cartimandua, apparently desperate to avoid conflict at any price, handed him over to the Romans in chains. There was total outrage. Her husband, Venutius, walked out on her and formed an anti-Roman resistance movement.

* * *

Spring, AD 61. At Atherstone, 25 miles south of the Trent, Boudicca is standing in her chariot, 'huge of frame, terrifying of aspect', spear in hand, and declaiming in a harsh voice:

> 'I am leading you into battle not as a queen to recover my kingdom and treasures, but as an ordinary woman determined to avenge the loss of her liberty and the rape of her daughters. The Romans must realize that it is a fight to the death. If you men wish to live on in slavery, then I, a mere woman, do not. Follow me now to victory or submit to the Roman yoke!'

Boudicca has already led a successful uprising in the south-east, and victory seems within her grasp. She appeals to Cartimandua for help, but what does Cartimandua do? Nothing. The 'warrior-queen' of the Brigantes, the supposed incarnation of Brigantia herself – who could have changed the whole course of British history – far from fulfilling her role as the goddess of war, stands by and watches as 80,000 men, women and children are systematically hacked to death. And then she dares to say that this only shows the folly of trying to oppose the might of 'the Unconquered' ...

THE BEGINNING OF THE END

A sorry time it was then for the next eight years. The People of the Peak were filled with shame, and many Roman soldiers in their garrisons were disgusted by what they had done. But Venutius's resistance movement gained little support. A kindlier regime under a new governor professed magnanimity, and those nobles who were pro-Roman, and impressed by the material comforts of Roman life, learned Latin and ridiculed the druids, who warned:

> '*Don't trust them one Roman pace!* Behind their smiling faces there is intrigue. Look at their road-building: the Rykneld Way is being widened and a "Long Lane" is being pushed westwards to Rocester. Step by step, pace by pace, the Romans are enclosing us, tightening the noose. Do they not know that if you prod a wild boar long enough it will suddenly turn on you with great ferocity?'

Which is exactly what happened. Wonderful news came to Nine Stones in AD 69 that Venutius had attacked Cartimandua's stronghold north of the Peak and overthrown her. There were glorious tales of Roman prisoners being disembowelled and burned alive as a sacrifice to Anu. But the druids were glummer than ever. This, they said, was a disaster: the Romans would never let Venutius stay in power. This was the beginning of the end. Expect the worst.

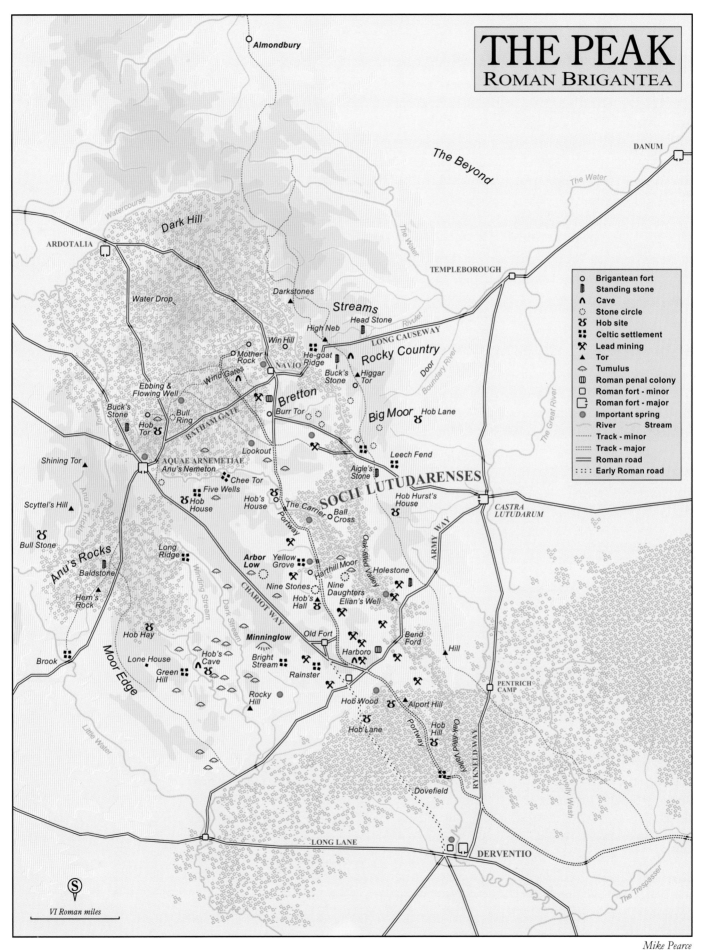

THE PEAK
ROMAN BRIGANTEA

Legend:

- ○ Brigantean fort
- ▯ Standing stone
- ∧ Cave
- ◌ Stone circle
- ⚥ Hob site
- ⚏ Celtic settlement
- ⚒ Lead mining
- ▲ Tor
- ⌒ Tumulus
- ▥ Roman penal colony
- ▢ Roman fort - minor
- ▣ Roman fort - major
- ● Important spring
- River ⎯⎯⎯ Stream
- ·········· Track - minor
- ⁝⁝⁝⁝⁝⁝ Track - major
- ⎯⎯⎯ Roman road
- ⁞⁞⁞⁞⁞ Early Roman road

Almondbury

The Beyond

DANUM

The Water

ARDOTALIA

Dark Hill

TEMPLEBOROUGH

Watercourse

Water Drop

Darkstones ▲

Streams

Head Stone

Rivulet

High Neb

LONG CAUSEWAY

Win Hill

He-goat Ridge

Rocky Country

Mother Rock

NAVIO

Buck's Stone

Higgar Tor

Door

Wind Gates

Bretton

Boundary River

Ebbing & Flowing Well

Burr Tor

Big Moor

Hob Lane

Buck's Stone

Bull Ring

Hob Tor

BATHAM GATE

Leech Fend

Shining Tor ▲

Lookout

AQUAE ARNEMETIAE

Anu's Nemeton

Aigle's Stone

SOCII LUTUDARENSES

Scyttel's Hill ▲

Chee Tor

Five Wells

Hob's House

CASTRA LUTUDARUM

Hob House

The Carrier

Ball Cross

Hob Hurst's House

Bull Stone

Anu's Rocks

Long Ridge

Arbor Low

Yellow Grove

Harthill Moor

Holestone

Baldstone

Nine Stones

Nine Daughters

Hem's Rock

Hob's Hall

Elian's Well

ARMY WAY

Hob Hay

CHARIOT WAY

Minninglow

Old Fort

Bend Ford

Hill ▲

Brook

Moor Edge

Lone House

Hob's Cave

Bright Stream

Rainster

Harboro

Green Hill

PENTRICH CAMP

Rocky Hill

Hob Wood

Alport Hill ▲

Hob Lane

Hob Hill

RYKNELD WAY

Oak-filled Valley

Little Water

Winding Stream

Dark Stream

Portway

Dovefield

Gravelly Wash

Ⓢ

VI Roman miles

LONG LANE

DERVENTIO

The Trespasser

Mike Pearce

THE BATTLE OF HARTINGTON MOOR

AD 72. Enormous cohorts of the notorious Twentieth Legion are marching briskly up the Old Portway from Derventio, each cohort consisting of six companies, each company about eighty men. Enormous men with big feet, marching six abreast with their shields on their backs. Helmeted, metal-clad, tight-lipped, hard-faced, purposeful, unstoppable; striding into the ancient fastness of the Peak with giant paces. Devouring the landscape with Roman 'miles', each mile a thousand double paces. The people of Alport Heights and Harboro fleeing before them. And then the gigantic column swinging leftwards on to the old trackway towards Minninglow to overrun the fort at Aldwark, where they encamp for the night.

It is at once obvious that their objective is Anu's Nemeton, the central township of the Peak. But the people are ready for them, and their long-hatched emergency plan goes into operation, to intercept the Romans on the high ground of Hartington Moor near Arbor Low. Against such an enormous foe every able-bodied person is involved, women included. From all around they come – from Cranes Fort and Calling Low, Bank Top and Smerrill Barn, Nine Stones Close and Castle Ring, Dark Stream and Bright Stream, Long Ridge and Yellow Grove, Wine's Thorn Bush and Badeca's Spring.

And so, by first light, a vast army has assembled on Lean Low overlooking the ancient trackway. Today will be the day of reckoning; today will decide if they are *subiecti* (servile) or *superbi* (proudly intransigent). Today, Sol Invictus, the Unconquered Sun, will face the wrath of the moon goddess.

The Romans have not been expecting either as large or as strange a force as this. It is an extraordinary sight: hundreds of semi-naked men wearing nothing but trousers and bearing a motley assortment of spears and swords. A shocking number have no shields at all. Some, indeed, are so proud of their physical endowments and their exotic body-painting as to be totally naked. And, all among them, their hair streaming in the wind, wild women, 'looking like the Furies', dart about with flaming torches, uttering unearthly war cries.

As the Romans spread out into battle formation, forming a line over a quarter of a mile wide, the Brigantes' war cries rise to a climax, urged on by a tremendous cacophony of trumpets and horns, while, up on the crest of Lean Low, the druids utter prayers and call down curses from Anu, flinging their arms towards the heavens.

For a moment the Romans seem paralysed with fear. Then suddenly they are charging forward into a hail of spears, which bounce ineffectively off their laminated wood and leather shields. But this is the moment the Brigantes have been waiting for: with nothing but their swords and blue-painted shields to protect them, they charge into battle – stark naked, bare-headed, howling and *superbi*.

The Roman line appears to hesitate, there is a shrill whistle, and before the Brigantes know what is happening the sky is full of missiles, as thousands of javelins rain down on them. Many of the Brigantes with shields find themselves suddenly encumbered with a seven-foot javelin impaled in the soft wood, while those without shields are felled at once. The few who are unscathed, still screaming their war cries, charge on regardless. Certain of immortality, they rush fearlessly upon the advancing steel; moving with lightning speed, slashing wildly with their swords, they leap nimbly among their hated foe, who look hot and overclad in their plate armour and iron helmets. Never before have the Romans experienced such ferocity, and for several bloody minutes the Brigantes make remarkable progress, even managing to hack off a few heads. One naked warrior

John Pickin

picks up a now helmetless head and, holding it by its hair, uses it as a terrifying new form of shield-cum-weapon. But it is a reckless bravery, for they are hopelessly outnumbered, and today the Romans have Fortuna and vastly superior tactics and equipment on their side.

The Roman wings charge forward on either flank making a V formation, and the Brigantes are suddenly forced together as two walls of rectangular shields close in on them like the jaws of death, with short, strong swords stabbing through the slits in the shield walls with lethal efficiency. Soon the Brigantes have not room even to swing their swords. Forced to thrust rather than slash, their weak blades are soon bent. Completely weaponless, some of the proud Peakmen wrestle with the Roman shields even as they are being stabbed, their blue body-painting being gaudily enriched with their own blood.

The remains of the Brigantean army are now fleeing for their lives – even back to the sacred ramparts of Arbor Low. All they have left for defence are slings and stones, and with these they put up a tremendous final barrage. But the 'unconquerable' Romans, grouped now into several tight packs, simply raise their shields over their heads and creep unstoppably towards them like a number of giant and deadly tortoises with the stones bouncing futilely off their hard leather backs. And then the air is full of cries of pain and anger, and the hack and crack of sword on bone. The wolves howl, the ravens croak, the skies darken, and all among the sacred standing stones the hot Brigantean blood sinks slowly back into the cool mother earth.

◀ Mam Tor in February

POST MORTEM

After this carnage there is little further resistance. Venutius is never heard of again, the hateful Cartimandua is reinstated, and the old regime is back. But everything has changed. Although the Brigantes are still officially an 'independent state', there are Romans everywhere. All the Brigantean forts, such as Aldwark, Castle Ring, Ball Cross, Mam Tor, Burr Tor and Higgar Tor – so recently strengthened under Venutius's rule – are now garrisoned by Romans.

One of the first tasks of the Romans is to suppress the Celtic religion. The druids who incited resistance are all taken away and executed, and Roman names are substituted for the Brigantean gods. Brigantia, Elian and Anu become 'the Matrones', and Hob becomes Mercury. And the ultimate humility – 'Behold the triumph!' – buildings with *baths* are constructed over the springs at Anu's Nemeton, and the whole township is renamed 'Aquae Arnemetiae'.

Meanwhile, supporters of Venutius and local convicts find themselves thrown together in unlikely road gangs to help the Roman soldiers upgrade the old trackway past Minninglow to Aquae Arnemetiae – and then extend it, via Batham Gate, to a new fort beside the Nav (now the River Noe), which they call 'Navio'. At the same time the Rykneld Way is pushed northwards from Derventio on the high ground east of the Derwent to another new fort or Castra at what is now Chesterfield. Everywhere there are Roman surveyors and road gangs as the network of roads encloses around them.

By AD 78 there is no longer any mention of Cartimandua; instead, an awful new name reverberates on every lip: *Julius Agricola*, the new governor of Britannia, cultivator of terror.

THE 'REWARDS OF VICTORY'

Spring, AD 79. The sound of chariot wheels and galloping horses, as literally hundreds of chariots hurtle up the road past Minninglow (now called the Chariot Way) and vast legions of marching soldiers bring the full weight of the Roman military machine into the Peak. And with them, new gods: the terrifying Jupiter, god of thunder and war, and Mars, the foot-soldier, god of battle. Any troublemakers are quickly rounded up and thrown into new penal colonies – near Navio in the north and Harboro in the south. Anybody disobeying an order is executed on the spot. The settlement at Nine Stones Close is razed to the ground with *ballistae* – enormous rock-hurling catapults – and the 39 great standing stones of Arbor Low are upturned with crowbars.

And then other roads of more mysterious purpose are built with extraordinary speed: first an 'Army Way' linking Chesterfield with Harboro, and then another running out north-westwards from Chesterfield over the high ground of the eastern edges – the township of Leech Fend being demolished in the process – and, fording the Derwent, up again on to the high ground of Eyam Edge past Burr Tor to Navio.

One day, along this new road, marching on foot with several cohorts, comes Agricola himself, helmeted and humourless. The people of Bretton, one of the heartlands of the Brigantes which has now become a virtual prison, watch sullenly, full of impotent loathing; and behind, escorted by Roman soldiers and overseen by a centurion wielding a stick, come straggling and shuffling – whatever next? – hundreds of slaves from far away across the seas, speaking in a strange dialect.

All too soon it becomes only too clear just what these cunning and duplicitous Romans have been planning all along. All these new roads and penal camps, these slaves and prisoners, are for one purpose only – called by Tacitus the 'rewards of victory' – a vast new lead-mining operation run from Chesterfield. The whole of the Peak becomes, in effect, one giant penal colony called Lutudarum, with its inhabitants *damnati in metalla* – condemned to the (metal) mines. Brigantea as a separate state has gone for ever; henceforth it is simply part of 'Britannia Inferior'.

Once again the miners plant rowans by the entrances to the mines – no longer through any desire that the lead should grow, but in the forlorn hope that even now Anu and Brigantia might come to their aid.

▶ Rowan berries below
Birchen Edge in late October

THE GODS FIGHT BACK

The People of the Peak never gave up hope, never gave in; indeed, by the mid-second century, when the military presence had been reduced, reports were reaching Rome that they had become aggressive, and that the wooden forts of Navio and Derventio had been burned to the ground. When they were rebuilt in stone, the uprisings only increased in intensity; and when German troops – of all people (given their close cultural links with the Celts) – were sent to repress them, they became mutinous and refused to obey orders.

In 208 Emperor Septimus Severus (who was not given that name without good reason) decided, in a surprising move, that the only way to control the situation was to let the Roman troops marry the natives, and within a few years his successor, Caracalla, had gone so far as to allow all free-born Britons to become Roman citizens. For the first time in 130 years the Peak people were no longer slaves. Rapid integration of the Roman and civilian population followed, bringing with it a period of prosperity and peace which was later called the 'Golden Age'. Luxurious Romano-British villas, using enormous amounts of lead for their plumbing, sprang up all around the chief mining areas of Carsington, Middleton and Bretton. Very pleased they were with their latest technology of pipes and cisterns.

Beneath Carsington Reservoir, created in 1990, lie the remains of several Roman villas which were clearly connected with the lead-mining operations around Harboro

The wealthy Romans who had intermarried soon became almost more British than the British and embraced the gods of the Old Religion with enthusiasm. The horned god regained his original name of Hob, and the ennead of moon-goddesses re-emerged as 'Apollo's nine ladies-in-waiting'. Yet what these Romano-British revivalists failed to grasp was that these were difficult gods who had been sorely abused. As Gibbon put it, 'Prosperity ripened the principle of decay'. There was raging inflation, extensive corruption, and over fifty emperors in as many years, many being murdered within days or months of taking office. And there were enormous logistical problems all along the vast borders of the empire. In Britain there were attacks from the north by Picts – Aquae Arnemetiae was probably razed at this time – and in the east by Saxons, and there were Germanic pirates on the high seas. Well before Rome was plundered by the Goths in 410, the Romans had abandoned Britain.

The old mother-goddess of the earth had regained her powers. The lead really *had*, in a sense, 'grown' – it had grown poisonous. As greedy *commercium* had led to decadence and hyperinflation, so the old gods had gone to work on the minds of the autocratic Roman rulers and turned them to jelly. Poisoned them with their very own 'spoils of victory'. The 'trespassers' had failed to learn one fundamental old truth: never underestimate the magic powers of these ancient rocks.

▶ Minninglow at sunset

3 Dark Ages

BORDER FOLK

What is often forgotten is just how enormous the time span was from the departure of the Romans to the Norman Conquest, it being rather longer than that from the Black Death (which reached the Peak in 1349) to the present day. We have to comprehend a vast period of transition and cultural darkness, of shifting boundaries and beliefs, a twilight zone in which a new order could but dimly be seen, and yet in which, without excessive bloodshed, the foundations of a modern, tolerant England were firmly established. Throughout this time, the Peak, being right at the wild heart of the country, was always at the centre of opposing forces. Always in between.

Into the political vacuum left by the Romans came barbarians from Europe – chiefly Angles from the far north of Germany. At first actually invited in by the Romano-British to help fight the Picts, they soon turned against them. And as the power struggle unfolded, ever greater numbers of Angles, hearing of 'the Britons' worthlessness and the choice nature of their land', arrived to add to the turmoil.

For a while the Peak was unaffected, with the Trent once again acting as a natural border. But by the middle of the sixth century the incomers had become bolder, and a large number of warrior-farmers were seen coming up the Derwent in their longboats. First they seized the old Romano-British fort of Derventio and then they encamped at a 'wide tract of land' at Duvafeld (Duffield). By 585 these Germanic settlers, who called themselves *Mierce*, 'border folk', had founded the kingdom of 'Mercia', with its capital at Repton and other major settlements at Esseburna (Ashbourne), Cesterfelda (Chesterfield) and Northworthy (North Enclosure) near Derventio.

Now they slowly began to infiltrate the Peak, principally west of the Derwent in the vicinity of 'The Street', as they called the old Roman Chariot Way, which was already grassing over from disuse. Calling themselves the 'Peak Settlers' *(Pecsaetna)*, these German intruders were bigger than the Romans, having even longer strides and bigger feet, and their miles were longer too. Once again we can imagine the British locals, intensely suspicious, watching and wondering; but there was no open conflict or resistance, for culturally these intruders were very similar to themselves. The Pecsaetna's chief god, Woden, was a magician-god of the Other World who appeared to have much in common with their own horned god, Hob/Mercury.

But there was one big difference. The Angles brought with them a whole new agrarian culture, based on the ox-drawn plough, with which they could rip up the mother earth on a grand scale and make a single 'open field' for a whole community. And, by Jupiter, were they arrogant! Everything, it seemed, had to be named after them. It was always somebody-or-other's enclosure or hamlet – 'Brand's people's township' (Brassington) or 'Tidsige's estate' (Tissington).

◀ Abbotside Farm and Chrome Hill in December

◀◀ Bonsall Moor in the grip of winter

35

THE RAM IN THE THICKET

Worse: arriving with these new farmers and their plough-dominated, patriarchal society were some real weirdos who talked mouthfuls of nonsense about 'one god', an all-male tyrant who had a cunning and devious son. And it was not just a double act: in a bizarre parody of their own triad of moon-goddesses, they insisted that he was a 'trinity' – of Father, Son and 'Holy Ghost' – the third element of which, when pressed, they could not explain. But the son was the one to watch, being full of clever sayings and some plainly daft notions like 'loving your enemy'.

Yet all this talk was highly contagious. In a context of uncertainty and change, in which Woden and Hob alike were losing their powers, a surprising number of people were seduced by it. The Old Religion had been failing them, with Tup, the ram-god of the spring, taking longer and longer to reach his appointed place with the sun-god at the equinox. Every two generations he had arrived a day later. Which meant that now, at the crucial midpoint between summer and winter when night exactly equalled day, the first point of his horns was no longer visible before sunrise, and his role of sun's consort had been taken by the effete and inconsequential Fishes. It was as if all the old gods of the zodiac were losing their way. The inescapable image they had was of an aged ram (or buck) caught up by his horns in a dense thicket, just as the old bull-god had become entangled in a thorn bush over two millennia before. Lost in a dark wood.

In this strange new atmosphere of doubt, death was no longer seen as a trivial incident in an eternal life but as a dark abyss in which life provided but a fleeting moment of security. One disillusioned old druid used the metaphor of a sparrow flying through a lighted house at night:

> In its little time indoors, the winter weather touches it not, yet its brief moment of security lasts but a second, as it passes from winter to winter. So seems the life of man in its little season; what follows, and what went before, we know not. Therefore, if this new teaching brings anything more certain, we should follow it.

A KINGDOM WITHIN A KINGDOM

In the High Peak, however, the people were not to be so easily swayed. Here, on the northern fringes of Mercia – in what amounted almost to a kingdom within a kingdom – the old Celtic *cymry* (countrymen) whom the Angles called the Brettons, remained true to their ancient beliefs and hunting culture.

The Bretton enclave of the High Peak was in effect an enormous natural fortress, a remote cul-de-sac surrounded by steep natural ramparts, with strategic forts and lookout posts on every high point – all along 'The Great Ridge' from Lose Hill to Mam Tor, and back the other side in a great arc, past Castle Hill, Burr Tor and The Freeman's Fortification (Carl Wark) – all the way to High Neb on Stone Edge. And right in the centre was their military seat of power, Thorn Hill.

Fully aware that they were now a buffer zone between the rival Anglian kingdoms of Mercia and Northumbria, and with the encouragement of the Mercian kings, the Brettons spent their time building dykes and defensive earthworks, such as Bar Dyke above the Loxley Valley in the far north-east and Grey Ditch across the Roman road of Batham Gate to defend their southern access route.

▶ The secretive enclave of Bretton Clough cloaked in autumn mist

WINNERS AND LOSERS

When, in 627, King Edwin of Northumbria was baptized as a Christian, the old rivalry between the two kingdoms took on a potent new religious dimension. The Mercian king, Penda, enlisted the help of Cadwallon, the military leader of Gwynedd, who shared his deep hatred of the Christians.

Exactly what happened next must remain pure speculation, but one very plausible scenario, which accords with both the legend and the known facts, is that Edwin's army entered the High Peak in 633 by the Roman road from the north-east over the Hallam Moors known as the Long Causeway and, after a major battle, took the all-important military stronghold of Thorn Hill, later called Win Hill. One can then imagine a stalemate with the rival forces facing each other across Edale for days or even weeks, with the 'winners' (the Northumbrians) on one hill and the 'losers' (the Mercians) on the other (though the oft-cited theory that this is the origin of the names of the respective hills is almost certainly far-fetched). All the time, the opposing armies would be amassing reinforcements on either side – with Penda's and Cadwallon's forces stationed at strategic points all along the southern boundary wall of the Bretton enclave effectively preventing any further penetration into Mercia from the north and yet unable to mount a counterattack with their forces so dispersed.

Eventually, perhaps in the dead of night, Edwin makes a foolhardy attempt to break through the cordon; but the enemy lookouts are sharp, and before they know what is happening Cadwallon's men are charging down Lose Hill behind them and – Brettons to right of them, Brettons to left of them, 'into the jaws of death, into the mouth of hell' – they are engulfed in front of the Grey Ditch. (The shallow knoll beside Navio where the battle would have started is perhaps appropriately called Folly Hill.) The bloody massacre that followed is commemorated for ever in the name of the section of Roman road which crosses the ditch: Gore Lane. Legend has it that Edwin was captured alive – and we are left with the awful image of him, unrepentant to the end, uttering strange prayers to Jesus even as they hanged him from a tree, with the slain all around him, just in front of the Ditch.

But for the Brettons it was a hollow victory. When the victorious Cadwallon pushed north into Northumbria – into that region beyond the Peak which they simply called Deira, The Beyond – he was soon defeated and killed, and any fanciful hopes they had of sharing power with the Angles were dashed for ever. Penda and his Mercian successors ruled supreme.

So it was that the German settlers of the Peak, numbering 1,200 'households' at the time of Penda, gained the upper hand. Being Angles in origin, they now called themselves 'the English', and they had the effrontery to call the Brettons – the native *cwmry* who had lived there for centuries – the *welisc* or Welsh, meaning *foreigners*. Thus were the Brettons condemned for ever to being strangers in their own land. Confined to the backwaters.

▶ Sunset on Win Hill at the autumn equinox

SAINTS AND 'HOODED ONES'

For the next 150 years the Mercian kings consolidated the English into a nation. When the Mercian dynasty was finally broken by King Ecgbert of Wessex in 826, it amounted to little more than a change of monarchy; and when, three years later, the Northumbrian King Eanred offered Ecgbert his obedience and allegiance at Dore, just north of the Peak border, it was the beginning of a united kingdom.

In theory the English nation was now Christian, but in the old Bretton enclave of the High Peak the people remained staunchly pagan. Monks who came literally from the back of 'beyond' (i.e. beyond Deira) in the late seventh century – from a place at the edge of the sea called Lindisfarne – were given a frosty welcome. Particularly distasteful to the Brettons was the concept of 'Saint Mary', by which the Celtic triad of creative and destructive mother-goddesses – representing the whole of womanhood – was sterilized and reduced to one single aspect: that of the pure, chaste virgin, the *virgo intacta*; just as the nine orgiastic daughters of the moon-goddess were now condemned for ever to be nine *virgins*.

The missionaries' treatment of the ancient springs which had been in the service of the water-goddess Elian – such as the one in Darley Dale beside the famous yew – was even worse. Deliberately, provocatively, they founded their new churches right next to them, and dedicated them to an entirely fictitious 'Saint Helen', who did not appear to do anything, except do what she was told. In time, Saint Helen's well at Wirksworth would become nothing more than the town's water supply. And perhaps most mortifying of all, at Arnemetum, the old sacred centre of the Peak, the potency of the horned god was fossilized into 'Buck's Stone' (Buxton), and the Aquae in its midst – Anu's great old wells of fertility – were dedicated to a fictional and insipid 'Saint Anne'.

It seems that, at best, the Peak people of the late Dark Ages were never more than reluctant converts. They were of the type amusingly described by Pennethorne Hughes, who had 'a habit of reappearing periodically for baptism for the sake of the baptismal robes awarded them as part of the ceremony'. 'Christianity' here inevitably remained a hybrid, a syncretism retaining many of the ancient pagan customs. Most of the Christian crosses dating from this period show a mixture of Christian artwork and pagan symbols, while an Anglo-Saxon warrior's helmet found at Benty Grange near Arbor Low has a Latin cross on its nosepiece and a boar, sacred to the pagan god Freyr, on its crest.

All the time, lurking in remote nooks and retreats in the hills and forests, far from the beaten tracks, the followers of the Old Religion, who had by now acquired the epithet of 'the hooded ones', remained attached to their old practices, worshipping the rocks and the trees and the horned god. And hunting.

The eighth-century Anglo-Saxon cross at Eyam, showing a mixture of Christian, Celtic and Norse symbolism

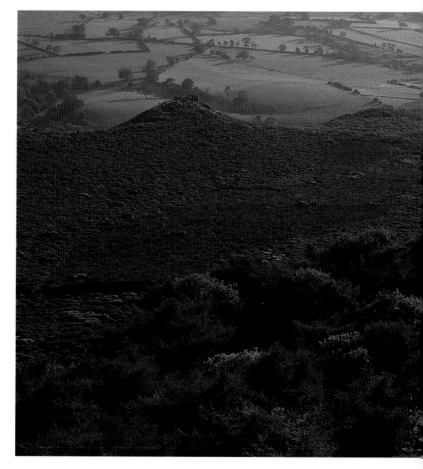

▶ Nooks and retreats in the Roaches above Five Clouds

ONE-EYED AND BONELESS

Just when it seemed, at the end of the eighth century, that stability (and Christianity) had been secured, the greatest scholar of the day, Alcuin, was warning of an immense new threat that 'hangs over this island and its people'. More pagans with horned helmets were arriving in their longboats from Europe: this time, Vikings from Denmark, with 'blue eyes and flowing hair' and calling themselves 'The Force'. One of their first targets was Lindisfarne, the centre of Christian learning, which they destroyed in 793. By 867 the whole of Northumbria had fallen to them, and Ivar the Boneless's 'Great Army' turned its attention to Mercia. As of old, there was a standoff for a while at the Trent, with the invaders setting up winter quarters in successive years at Nottingham and Repton, and 'making peace' with the locals. But it was short-lived; in 874 they seized power from the English at Repton and started to move into the Peak.

Although the Vikings are traditionally represented as the very epitome of terror, it seems that by the time they arrived in the Peak they had acquired a much gentler demeanour. Indeed, it has been argued by Theodore Zeldin that, unlike the Brettons, they had a great fear of mortality. For them the only thing that was immortal was their reputation, and for that it was necessary first of all to show complete self-control. (Perhaps the English stiff upper lip has come from Scandinavia all along?) In a very modern and egalitarian way they believed that everybody could achieve fame, because everybody had equal authority, and that no one should take orders from anyone.

With their independent nature and their strong aversion to the Christian Church and its symbols, one can imagine the Brettons warming to the Danes. Their main god, Odin, was identical to the Saxon Woden and Celtic Hob, except that he lived in Valhalla with some helmeted women called Valkyries who rushed about in space on fiery chargers. One-eyed and vulnerable, he used trickery and magic as much as physical strength in order to survive. Like Hob, he could shape-shift, changing in an instant into a bull, a bird, a snake or a monster. Which, given the range of his duties – he was at once god of war, wisdom, poetry, agriculture and the dead – was certainly a great asset.

Such was their skill in adaptability that an amicable agreement was reached in 878 whereby the Anglo-Saxons would keep the west of England and the Danes the east. The Peak, as so often in its history, was once again a borderland, with the boundary now running roughly north–south along the line of the Old Portway. The Danes gained the strategically important settlements of Northworthy on the Derwent – which they renamed Deoraby (Derby, 'the farmstead where deer are kept') – and Wirksworth on the Old Portway. At Nine Stones the Mercians kept the Castle Ring and the land west of the Portway, while the Danes gained Badecanwella (Bakewell) and the land east of the Portway. At a local level it is perhaps not too far-fetched to imagine them sealing their agreement up on Holestone Moor, near Matlock, using once more the old and very sacred Holestone (see Chapter 1, p.8). Only now they would be performing the 'Promise of Odin', the most binding of all oaths for the Vikings, by clasping hands through the hole in the rock.

So it was that all down the eastern slopes of the Peak, especially on the high ground above the Rother and its tributaries, and in the Bretton heartland around Edale and Hathersage, these Scandinavians who had come as pirates settled down as easy-going farmers.

◄ Looking south over Mermaid's Pool and the western flanks of Peaclond from Kinder Scout. Local folklore has it that the pool is bottomless and that the mermaid may still be seen swimming here at midnight on the eve of Easter Sunday

'PEACELAND'

This amicable state of affairs lasted for less than forty years. In 917 the Mercians fought to regain the Peak; in particular they wanted back Bakewell and Derby. A century of turbulence followed, with first Derby, and then the whole of England, changing hands three times, before the Anglo-Saxon kingdom was restored in 1042 by King Edward the Confessor.

The picture we have of the Peak at this stage in history, called since 924 Peaclond (one spelling even has it as 'Peaceland'), is of a peaceful, moderately ordered society consisting of a diverse mixture of highly adaptive peoples from central and northern Europe: Celts, Romans, Germans and Scandinavians. If not always the friendliest of neighbours, certainly living in relative harmony; if belonging already to a feudal system, still maintaining considerable freedom, for there was a new class of independent farmers ('socmen') who worked their land separately from the village; and, if they were Christians at all, only in the sense of a very broad and tolerant Church in which much of the indigenous Celtic culture and practices had been allowed to survive.

The start of the new millennium also ushered in a new phase of hot, almost Mediterranean weather, the finest since the Bronze Age. The Derwent woodlands became a more attractive environment than ever in which to live. This was a land flowing not so much with milk and honey as with venison and wine, for vineyards, even in the valleys of the High Peak, were commonplace.

But, as so often in history, such moments of benignity are all too fleeting. On the eve of the old Celtic fire festival of Beltaine (1 May) in 1048, a great earthquake shook southern Peaclond, and a contemporary chronicler noted that there was great loss of life to men and livestock, and that 'the wildfire did much evil in the shire'. It was of course seen as a terrible portent. And not without good reason: for the very man who had brought peace and stability to the region, King Edward, failed in one absolutely critical respect, which was to change the whole course of English history. He failed to produce an heir. And one of the claimants to the throne was a certain William, Duke of Normandy – who, as Conqueror, would be for the Peak people, as for the whole nation, a calamity without equal in our history.

4 Hunter and hunted

Those of the English who were of gentle birth were driven from their lands; they could not dig, to beg they were ashamed. So with their kindred they took refuge in the woods, living by what they could hunt, and only falling back on raiding when all else failed them … In their lairs in the woods and waste places they laid a thousand secret ambushes and traps for the Normans.

From the thirteenth-century chronicle, *The Flowers of History*

THE DEVIL'S ARSEHOLE

In 1068, two years after the Battle of Hastings, having ruthlessly crushed all resistance in the south, William crossed the Trent and took Derby and Snotingham – 'the homestead of the followers of a man called Snot' (Nottingham). Then, leaving his bastard son William Peverel to erect a castle on the rock there and to do his dirty work for him in Derbyshire, William the Bastard went north to Euruic (York).

South Derbyshire, it seems, offered little resistance, but in the Peak things were different. At Hortedun (Hartington), not far from the spot where their Celtic ancestors had been crushed by the Romans ten centuries before, the people put up an equally brave and futile fight – which resulted not only in their village being flattened, but the whole manor of Pilesberie (Pilsbury) and its outlying 'shelters' (Sheen) being laid waste too. Where the Romans had at least been rational (and clever), these Norman mercenaries were mad – so mad that they actually believed that 'Christ was on their side'. The repressive, fear-based brand of 'Christianity' they brought with them was full of extraordinary new doctrines, at once threatening and incomprehensible, mostly concerning 'hell' and punishment and a 'final judgement'. Certainly, they seemed hell-bent now on creating a hell on earth, as they went about imposing a tyranny that far exceeded anything the Romans had achieved.

Wherever there was resistance, it was the same story: Peverel would have the people driven from their homes and whole villages destroyed. Hundreds of manors were seized from their Saxon owners and redistributed among the Norman 'nobles'. A small amount of land was left in the hands of the original Saxon owners (once they had sworn an oath of fealty to William) as part of a deliberate policy to forestall further trouble. In addition, this foreign despot who acted as if he were God gave a quarter of the land to the Church – partly to guarantee his entry into the kingdom of heaven, but chiefly to strengthen his political stranglehold. The bishops, in their new role of feudal lords, depended on royal support to help them against their embittered neighbours, and this involved much grovelling. Most of the early monasteries, while being dedicated to the 'Holy Trinity', were also invariably 'devoted to praying for the souls of King William I and his consort Matilda'.

◀ Peace was shattered here in about 1070 when the manor of Pilsbury was seized by the Normans. Thirty years later a timber motte and bailey castle was built at the spot where this picture was taken to form the administrative centre for the Dove Valley

The resulting centralized hierarchy under the monarch was the most highly feudalized regime in Europe, vastly strengthening the weak feudal system which had already been in place. Many of the disinherited Saxon landlords held lands under extortionate mortgages to the Church or were forced to become tenant farmers on land that was classified as 'waste' (either as a result of William's 'scorched earth policy' or because the land was so poor that it was considered unsuitable for farming). Their lot was little better than that of William Langland's 'poor ploughman': 'while the Friars feast on roast venison, they have bread and thin ale, with perhaps a scrap of cold meat or stale fish'.

Those who had never been landowners (over a third of the population) were *villeins*, tenants who had to work for the lord and were not allowed to leave the district without his consent. A term which had originally meant a 'free villager' soon came to signify nothing more than a low-born, malevolent wretch, and by the seventeenth century had acquired the criminal connotations of the modern word 'villain'.

The census of 1085 known as the Domesday Book (from the word *dom,* 'judgement'), in which whole communities were re-evaluated, was a detailed summary of the Normans' spoils – and spoil things they surely had. Almost every manor in Derbyshire – from Horsley to Hereseige (Hathersage) – had been halved in value. 'Doomsday' had indeed been a 'day of reckoning', a last judgement which sealed the people's fate for generations.

Part of the land that William had assigned to his bastard son, the so-called 'Honor of Peverel', included the manor and forest of the High Peak. The 'Castle of the Peak' (*Castelli de Pech*) which Peverel built on Castle Hill in 1069 was aptly described by the historian Thierry as being 'perched on a rock like the nest of a foul bird of prey'. It would be nice to think that the Peak Cavern (directly below the castle) got its original name, *Pechesers*, the Peak's Arse, or Devil's Arsehole, from what the locals thought of the Norman regime in general and Peverel in particular.

The delightful story of the goose which was seen to fly down Eldon Hole and emerge from the Peak Cavern at Castleton without a single feather on its back must reluctantly be dismissed as a fable

J B Firth

◄ Looking directly up out of the mouth of Peak Cavern, the 'Devil's Arsehole'

◀ Woods below Beeley Moor in November

HUNTERS OF MEN

The construction of Peak Castle marked the beginning of a more sinister development. As if life had not been made bad enough already, these dangerous and unpleasant foreigners – when they were not away on the other side of the world on fanatical religious crusades – were obsessive hunters; and as part of a nationwide policy of 'afforestation', in which a third of the land in England was taken over as 'King's Forests', a vaguely defined area that had previously been used for hunting by the Saxon kings was now set aside as the 'Royal Forest of the Peak'. In open contempt for the ancient woodland rights of 'grazing and gleaning', some 200 square miles of some of the wildest and highest country in Derbyshire, bounded by the Rivers Wye, Goyt, Etherow and Derwent, were sealed off from the local people. Under the new 'Forest Law', the forest-dwellers who had lived there for centuries were cut off from their traditional livelihood. Unable to hunt on their own land, and with deer grazing at will and wolves taking their sheep, these age-old hunting people were forced to abandon their farms and hamlets.

The new word 'forest', denoting hunting territory, had nothing to do with woods as such – as is clear from such expressions as 'woods within the forest'. Much of the 'Forest of the Peak' was wild moorland with patches of ash and oak woods and large open spaces that were perfect for the chase. The term 'forest' is probably derived from *foris*, meaning 'outside' – not just outside the village but, specifically, *outside the common law*.

The restrictions imposed by this new Law were outrageous. No dogs were allowed in the forest, and only bona fide travellers – who were restricted to the main trackways – were allowed to carry weapons of any kind. The Norman barons who remained within the forests, while gaining little from the system themselves, bore the brunt of the inevitable hatred.

Since Snotinghamshire and Derbyshire was one administrative area run by the king's personal representative, the Sheriff of Snotingham, the Sherwood and Peak Forests both came under the jurisdiction of the 'Justices of the Forest North of the Trent'. The

Chief Forester of Peak Forest, with a team of twenty wardens and inspectors under him, ruled with absolute and arbitrary powers from a base in the centre (now the village of Peak Forest). The system soon degenerated into an extortionate business involving fines and protection money, which Simon Schama has aptly described as 'sylvan gangsterism'.

The Foresters, dubbed by one chronicler 'hunters of men', had the right to arrest anyone 'trespassing against verte and venyson' (trees and deer). Offenders were held in the Castle of the Peak until such time as the forest courts, called 'eyres', met at Tideswelle, Castelton or Hope. The penalties were vicious: there were massive fines for those found in possession of bows, arrows or dogs within the forest, or for trying to sell wood. For killing deer, amputation was the rule – first of ears or fingers and then, for subsequent offences, of the complete hand, the whole arm, and finally the feet.

The Laws became even harsher under Henry II who, according to one chronicler, 'was addicted to the chase beyond measure; at crack of dawn he was off on horseback, traversing waste lands, penetrating forests and climbing the mountaintops …' This madman, who wore a sprig of broom in his hat, perversely extended the Royal Forests well beyond anything that was suitable for hunting. When Peverel's great-grandson was charged in 1153 with 'foul conspiracy' for poisoning the Earl of Chester, Henry confiscated his estates and made the Peak Castle his personal hunting-lodge. He came here several times in his reign to ensure that his laws were being properly enforced – retrospectively if need be, so that sons were punished for crimes committed by their deceased fathers. The penalty for killing a deer was now death for a third offence. If no culprit was found, the nearest township would be held responsible and fined accordingly. From one forest eyre alone, £12,305 was raised. Any transgressor who failed to appear at an eyre – a common enough occurrence, given the penalties – would be outlawed, which meant that he then became an outcast from society, literally outside the law's protection, and with no more rights than a hunted beast.

It is fitting that the Armorial Bearings of Derby, which got its first charter from Henry II, should feature as its central motif 'the buck in the park' – a stag at rest between two oak trees, surrounded by a circular fence. It is the perfect symbol for the way in which the whole hunting culture of the Peak had been closed off from the people. The buck, the antlered god of the Old Religion, was now entrapped, not in a thicket, but behind the palings of a 'royal park'.

◀ Fallinge Edge and Beeley Plantation in November

▶ The Buck in the Park emblem in Derby Cathedral, painted in 1725

FOREST DESPERADOES

The Forest Law could not entirely destroy the ancient culture of the High Peak; it simply drove it underground, into the fastnesses of the Derwent woods and the eastern edges. Here, in forest hideouts and in clearings such as Ronksley ('Proud Man's Clearing') in the upper Derwent Valley – and all along the high rampart of the eastern edges from Stanage in the north to Birchens in the south, and eastwards down the Barlow, Holme and Hipper Valleys to the western fringes of Sherwood Forest – the outlawed and the dispossessed found their natural sanctuary. Stanage Edge was particularly favoured because this was the county border, and the wild district beyond, called Hallamshire (literally, a 'shire-within-a-shire'), lay outside the jurisdiction of the Sheriff of Snotingham.

Outlaws could hide very easily; there was little risk of being betrayed, because of the fines that this would bring on an entire community. The Hathersage (He-goat Ridge) area was a place where you did not ask questions and did not volunteer information if asked. The wilder parts of the forests and moorlands – described by one contemporary as places of 'terror and vast solitude' – were given a wide berth by most ordinary people, being the home not just of dangerous, impoverished outlaws but of wild boars, cats and bulls, and even bears.

For the wealthy baron or churchman, travelling across this country was extremely risky. All the main trackways over the high ground from Chestrefelde (Chesterfield), for example – such as the Arwey to Matlac (Matlock), and the Rykneld Way to Derby – were notorious for robbery, while, to the west of the Derwent, there was a particularly dangerous section on the Old Portway between Bathecwelle (Bakewell) and Wirkiswrthe (Wirksworth). It was generally advisable to travel fast, on horseback, and in large groups, because the robbers worked in gangs.

All the time, poaching in the Royal Forests was on the increase. Indeed it had become so widespread by 1198 that Richard I decreed that the punishment for killing any deer would henceforth be the 'removal of the offender's eyes and testicles'. But to little effect. It seems that the *illegal hunt*, the chasing and killing of the king's deer, had been elevated by its very prohibition into a thrilling and dangerous new 'sport' in its own right. It was almost a 'tournament', in which hot-headed desperadoes tried to beat the royal warlord at his own game. And with a completely clear conscience – for had they not had their *lands* poached?

BLACK AND WHITE ISSUES

On Richard's death in 1199, his younger brother, the new King John, made a surprising move: he granted the Upper Derwent estate (most of the Ronksley Valley) to the 'White canons' of Welbeck Abbey. At first it seemed that this was a clever ploy to dampen the brigandry, for the closeness with which some elements of the Church – notably the 'Black canons' of the Augustinian order – worked with the Crown to uphold 'Forest Justice' cannot be overemphasized. By doing so they gained special privileges within the Royal Forests: for example, a tithe of meat and hides when the king and his party were resident at Peak Castle. The widely detested Abbot of Darley not only had fishing rights on the Derwent but also his own forester and his own court.

But it soon emerged that the 'White canons' of the Premonstratensian order were entirely different, having a much more austere lifestyle and beliefs. They had sought

Ronksley ('Proud Man's Clearing') as it appears today, bereft of trees

out the remote Ronksley Valley through their straightforward love of solitary places where they could engage in sheep-farming free from manipulation by the Crown. The small abbey and two granges which they built on the east banks of the Derwent just outside the Peak Forest were rarely visited by local bishops. So it was that the embittered and proud Men of the Clearing suddenly found themselves with highly principled neighbours who, so far as was Christian, loathed the Black monks and bishops for their corruption and licentiousness no less than they did.

Perhaps most despised of all, because of his rapacious dealings with the locals, was the notorious Cellarer, who handled Darley Abbey's business affairs, buying and selling land and managing rents and mortgages. He was also responsible for Darley's supplies of food, ale and wine, which meant having to make frequent visits to the abbey's granges in the Peak.

But who are these travellers on horseback, coming up the Old Portway towards us past the Nine Stones … wearing black habits, their horses laden with provisions? … Why, it is our old friends, the Black monks from Darley!... and in their midst – by dear worthy God! – it is none other than the High Cellarer! They are drawing closer now; slowly, casually, carelessly, the horses shaking their heads, bothered by flies, the monks chattering profanely and laughing, their eyes closed to their surroundings, and looking remarkably relaxed for affluent 'men of God' travelling in dangerous parts in such a small group …

... apparently oblivious of the notorious landmark looming ahead ...

'BEND YOUR BOWS!' said Lytell Johan,
'Make all yon company stand!
The foremost monk, his life and his death
Is closed in my hand!

'Abide, churlish monk,' said Lytell Johan,
'No further that thou go;
If thou doest, by dear worthy God,
Thy death is in my hand!
And evil thrift on thy head! —
Right under thy hatty's band!'

'Who is your master?' said the monk.
Lytell Johan said, 'Robyn Hode.'
'He is a strong thief,' said the monk,
'Of him heard I never good.'

'Thou lyest!' then said Lytell Johan,
'And that thou shalt rue thee;
He is a yeoman of the forest,
To dine he hath bidden thee ...'

... They made the monk to wash and wipe,
And sit at his dinner,
Robyn Hode and Lytell Johan
They served him both in fare.

'Ye be the more welcome,' said Robyn,
'So ever may I thrive!
Fill of the best wine!' said Robyn,
'This monk shall drink to me!'

The monk swore a full great oath,
A sorry face had he ...

Lytell Johan spread his mantle down
(As he had done many times before)
And counted out from the monk's mailbag
Eight hundred pounds and more.

'By Our Lady!' then said the monk,
'That were no courtesy—
To bid a man to dinner,
And then him beat and bind.'
'—It is our old manner,' said Robyn,
'To leave but lytell behind!'

From the ballad *A Gest of Robyn Hode*, c.1400

ROBIN HOOD OF THE PEAK

The favoured theory now among scholars is that the original Robin Hood – despite recent attempts to resite him in Yorkshire a century later – was operating in Sherwood, with the Sheriff of Nottingham as his chief opponent, in the early part of the thirteenth century; and that he was so notorious that soon after his death, in about 1247, robbers all over England were emulating him and adopting the compound nickname 'Robynhod'.

It is my contention, based on considerable research, that the 'Peak District Robin Hood', after whom many local landmarks are named, is one and the same as the original, Sherwood outlaw. The bare bones of my hypothesis are that Robin Hood was born in Loxley, west of the small township of Scafeld (Sheffield) in Hallamshire, in around 1180. In 1198, after killing his (Norman?) stepfather – possibly as a result of a landowning dispute – he went into hiding, escaping up Loxley Chase into the wildest parts of the Hallam Moors around the Derwent and Stanage Edges. He was shortly thereafter outlawed and became the natural leader of the many outlaws living in the upper Derwent Valley and the eastern moors, and formed them into a kind of forest resistance movement. His right-hand man was the local strongman, 'Little John' of Hathersage, who knew intimately all the secret ways into Sherwood Forest ('... Little John to merry Sherwood, The paths he knew each one'). And then, for a 'Full thirteene yeares, and something more, These northerne parts he vexed full sore'.

Based in secret hideaways *between* the Peak and Sherwood Forests, Robin Hood and his 'merrie men' made frequent forays into each, with a dual strategy of poaching and robbery; but, in summer, their main theatre of operations would have been Sherwood, for this was right on the doorstep of the royal 'power centre' of Nottingham Castle and Robin's arch-enemy, the sheriff.

Like a cross between a nomadic hunter-warrior and a modern New Age 'traveller', at odds with the establishment and the law, Robin was always on the move. Never staying at one base for very long, and with an efficient 'jungle telegraph' system, he was always one step ahead of the Foresters and Justices. Sometimes after a particularly daring operation he 'stayed quiet for many a day', hiding high on the Hallam Moors, in caves on Stanage Edge or, perhaps most secret of all, at the upper end of the very remote and secluded valley of Abbey Brook a few miles up behind the Premonstratensian abbey.

▶ Abbey Brook at dusk in late November

◀◀ Pub sign, Robin Hood Inn, Baslow

THE GREEN MAN RULES OK

> So courteous an outlaw as he was one
> Was never none yfound.
>
> From the ballad *A Gest of Robyn Hode*, c. 1400

Perhaps it is in the Robin Hood ballads that we see for the first time in England an attack on undeserved privilege, and a demand for a fairer distribution of wealth (although it must be said that despite the popular, modern version of the legend, only on one occasion in the ballads does Robin Hood specifically rob the rich *in order* to give to the poor). What he apparently detests most of all is lack of *curtesye* – the arrogant disrespect shown by the new landowning classes for the People of the Forest. It seems that for him the chief virtues are audacity, courtesy and charity; but that the greatest of these is courtesy. For to be courteous was part of what it was to be a 'good yeoman', whose status lay somewhere between a *husbonde* (a labourer) and a gentleman. Before the middle class existed, Robin was a spokesman neither for a peasants' revolt nor quite for a barons' revolt, but something in between, which found allies in both camps.

But Robin was far more than just a public-spirited yeoman; he was the wild huntsman, Herne the Hunter, Hob incarnate. His followers met, as the druids had of old, around a great oak. It was always very secret: in the seclusion of the Proud Man's Clearing in the Valley of Oaks he was the Green Man personified, the Keeper of the Wood with its own anarchic moral code, holding sway under the 'chosen, trusty tree'. And, appropriately enough – on at least one occasion in the ballads – Robin Hood and his men dressed in green; and again, when Little John infiltrated Nottingham Castle in disguise, the pseudonym he adopted was 'Reynolde Grenelefe'.

As 'king' of the outlaws and downtrodden 'yeomen of the Forest', Robin Hood is a surrogate monarch, a rival chieftain upholding the ancient liberties of the greenwood. As Green Man he is both King of the Forest and Lord of the Jest, dedicated to undermining the inequities and iniquities of the Forest Law and the feudal state: here jurisprudence meets impudence, and arbitrary proclamations come face to face with magic powers. The Robin Hood ballads are full of the old pagan themes of shape-shifting, disguise and trickery. Real justice (and real *Christian* values, for that matter) are best served by ridiculing all the leading players of the new regime, whether they be Black monks, 'Justices', the sheriff or even the king himself.

Above all, Robin revels in *shaming* contests. For, at the end of the day, it is a test of 'Forest prowess'. The quest, the 'chase', is first and foremost about establishing who is the real 'king': the Green Man or the Royal Warlord, archetype or autocrat, prototype or pretender. In the English greenwoods, where longbow skills are honed which will shortly lead to success on the battlefields of France, the best archer, the best shot, is basically king. The hunt in the Royal Forest is a symbolic blood ritual to establish who is the real master. Who really is the hunter, who the hunted? The king and his deer or Robin, who, like Herne the Hunter, complete with horns, is both?

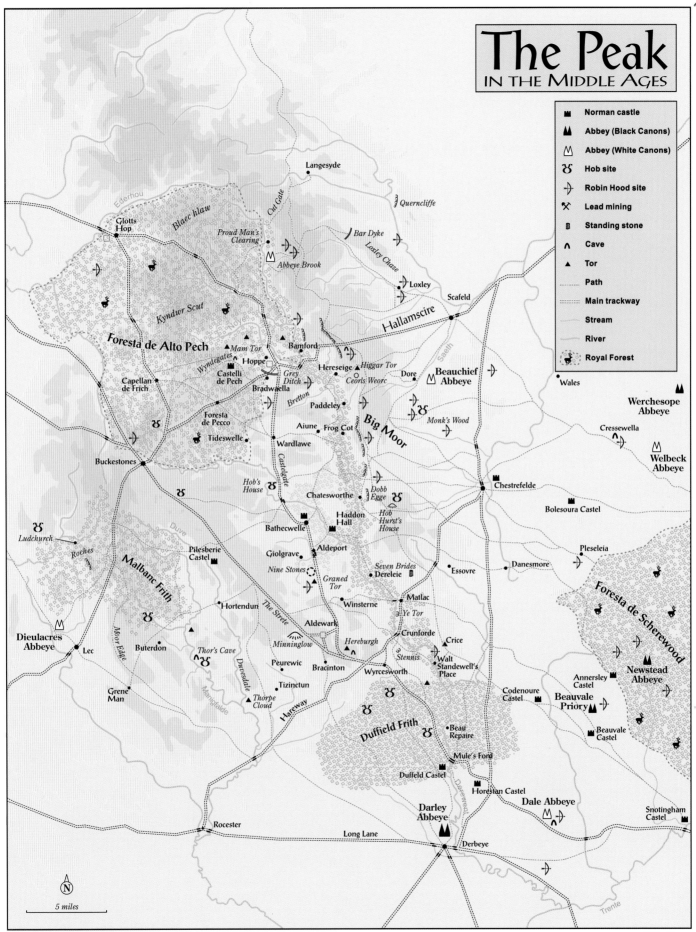

The Peak
IN THE MIDDLE AGES

	Norman castle
	Abbey (Black Canons)
	Abbey (White Canons)
	Hob site
	Robin Hood site
	Lead mining
	Standing stone
	Cave
	Tor
	Path
	Main trackway
	Stream
	River
	Royal Forest

Langesyde

Querncliffe

Ederhou

Glotts Hop

Blaec hlaw

Cut Gate

Proud Man's Clearing

Bar Dyke

Loxley Chase

Abbeye Brook

Loxley

Scafeld

Kyndwr Scut

Hallamscire

Foresta de Alto Pech

Mam Tor

Bamford

Hoppe

Hereseige

Higgar Tor

Dore

Beauchief Abbeye

Wales

Werchesope Abbeye

Wyndegates

Castelli de Pech

Grey Ditch

Ceorls Weorc

Capellan de Frich

Bradwaella

Bretton

Welbeck Abbeye

Paddeley

Monk's Wood

Cressewella

Foresta de Pecco

Aiune

Frog Cot

Big Moor

Tideswelle

Wardlawe

Welbeck Abbeye

Buckestones

Castelgate

Hob's House

Chatesworthe

Dobb Egge

Chestrefelde

Bolesoura Castel

Pleseleia

Hob Hurst's House

Haddon Hall

Bathecwelle

Danesmore

Ludchurch

Roches

Pilesberie Castel

Giolgrave

Aldeport

Nine Stones

Seven Brides

Dereleie

Essovre

Foresta de Scherewood

Malbanc Frith

Graned Tor

Matlac

Hortendun

The Strete

Winsterne

Ye Tor

Crunforde

Crice

Annersley Castel

Newstead Abbeye

Dieulacres Abbeye

Lec

Moor Edge

Buterdon

Thor's Cave

Minninglow

Hereburgh

Stennis

Walt Standewell's Place

Wyrcesworth

Codenoure Castel

Beauvale Priory

Beauvale Castel

Dovesdale

Peurewic

Bracinton

Grene Man

Tizinctun

Thorpe Cloud

Hareway

Duffield Frith

Beau Repaire

Mangfelde

Mule's Ford

Duffeld Castel

Horestan Castel

Dale Abbeye

Snotingham Castel

Rocester

Long Lane

Darley Abbeye

Derbeye

Dareneford

Trente

N

5 miles

In summer, when the woods be bright
And leaves be large and long
It is full merry in fair forest
To hear the birdes song:

To see the deer draw to the dale,
And leave the hilles high,
And shade themselves in the green leaves,
Under the greenwood tree.

From the ballad *Robin Hood and the Monk*, c.1450

◄ Ancient woodland below
Gardom's Edge

◄◄ Dovedale in mid-November

5 From Hob to Hobbes

Remember the cruelties!

Voltaire

THE LORD OF MISRULE

The great bubonic plague called the Black Death, which reached the Peak in May 1349, wiped out as much as half the population. In some hamlets – such as Smerrill Grange near Youlgreave, Uppertown near Birchover, and three settlements in Chatsworth Park – the loss of life was total, and they simply reverted to farmland. While the Church elders were busy blaming heretics and Jews, the majority of the people calmly persevered with their age-old pagan practices. At Tissington, where they kept faith with the ancient water-goddesses, the springwater protected them from contagion. It was pure Celtic magic. The village was completely spared and the next year, on Ascension Day (the nearest Christian feast-day to the old spring festival of Beltaine), they dressed their five wells with flowers as a token of thanksgiving.

All through the Middle Ages, the Old Religion persisted in the depths of the Derwent and Peak Forests. The Green Man still lurked in such secret hide-outs as the dark chasm of 'Ludchurch' in the densely wooded hillside above the Dane Valley, the very same 'Green Chapel' in which Sir Gawain hacked off the Green Knight's foliate head, as told in a famous fourteenth-century verse romance. And in Demon's Dale, at the outcrop called Hob's House near Monsal Head, Tup the Ram was still sacrificed at the solstices.

Under the Tudors, who were of Celtic (Welsh) descent, the May Day festival of Beltaine was transformed from a surreptitious gathering into a great public holiday which incorporated elements of the Robin Hood legend. Henry VIII would himself dress up as Robin Hood, and his nobles, 'clothed all in grene, with hodes on their heddes', would serve him and his queen, Catherine of Aragon, a breakfast of venison and wine in the woods 'to their great contentation'. Robin Hood's Maytime was a kind of pact between the sovereign and his people, an alternative Eastertide which represented the resurrection of pagan justice over monastic corruption. As the 'Lord of Misrule' at the 'May Games', Robin was, in the trenchant words of Simon Schama, a 'bringer of healing havoc'. Once, when a bishop tried to preach, he was given short shrift: 'Syr, thys is a busye daye wyth us, we can not heare you, it is Robyn Hoodes day.'

The real 'Lord of Misrule' was, of course, the increasingly overweight and paranoid Henry VIII; for this wife-swapper and serial killer, who saw himself as 'God's own deputy', was nothing if not a bringer of havoc. When he decided in 1529 to separate the English Church from Rome (because the Pope refused to allow him to divorce

◀ The wooded slopes of the Derwent around Padley Manor

Catherine of Aragon), he enlisted the support of the 'zely people', the Protestant zealots who regarded the Pope as the 'whore of Babylon'. Hastily decrying the monasteries as dens of corruption and sanctuaries of traitors, he proceeded to close them down between 1536 and 1540. The people of Buckstones (Buxton) watched in horror as first St Anne's Well, that most sacred place of pilgrimage for the sick, was locked up and its 'idol' smashed, and then the adjoining chapel, where those who had been cured had hung up their crutches, was demolished. Darley Abbey was likewise razed to the ground and the land surrendered to the Royal Commissioners, Thomas Legh and William Cavendish.

Henry's financial difficulties were such that most of the £2million-worth of monastic lands he gained had immediately to be sold off to the wealthy and the favoured. The aforementioned William Cavendish not only received much of the land he had helped to purloin, but was also appointed Treasurer of the King's Chamber. It is not perhaps surprising that while he was buying and completely rebuilding Chatsworth Manor House with his new wife, Bess of Hardwick, the enormous sum of £5,000 went missing from the Royal Chamber.

In fairness it should be said that part of the land acquired by the Cavendishes included Buckstones, and it was largely at Bess's instigation that, within thirty years, pilgrims were once again enjoying the 'Benefits of the Auncient Bathes'. Among the ailments that a contemporary physician, John Jones, claimed the water would cure were 'rickets, inflammations, fevers and rheums, headaches, weak sinews, old scabs, ulcers, cramps, numness, itchings, ringworms, impostumes, apoplexies, palsies, vertigo, melancholy, hypochondriack winds, jaundice, dropsie, sciatica, gout, asthma's, leprosie, dysentery, and hysteric passions ...'

In the last respect, at least, Dr Jones was sadly mistaken, for nothing could dampen the hysteric passions of the 'Reformation', as the 'zely people' vilified pagans, 'witches' and Catholics alike. Now that the Pope's authority had been rejected, the cry went up to 'Get rid of the poison with the author'.

◄ Hob's House, Monsal Dale

Ashop Clough below Kinder
northern edge

FIRE AND BRIMSTONE

As the weather became progressively colder and stormier, so the religious climate became
ever more turbulent, and the old, deeply ingrained Celtic tradition of balance seemed
irretrievably lost. The headlong, headstrong thrust of the Reformation had pushed the
pendulum of intolerance dangerously far; and when Henry VIII's daughter, the devout
Catholic, Mary Tudor, ascended the throne in 1553, it came crashing violently back
with the Counter-Reformation. Now it was the turn of the Catholics to reveal their
capacity for barbarism. Hundreds of Protestant heretics were burned at the stake, and
in arguably the most shameful hour in the whole history of Derbyshire, the 21-year-old
Joan Wast, who had been blind since birth, was burned in Derby for her beliefs, having
first heard the Diocesan Chancellor equate her physical blindness with 'blindness in
the eyes of her soul'.

The reign of 'Bloody Mary', as Queen Mary was later called, lasted only five years,
but in that time she managed to wreak havoc no less effectively than her homicidal
father. Bells and bonfires understandably greeted her death in November 1558. But
they were hysterical bells, for the pendulum of bigotry now came crashing back with a
vengeance. But Elizabeth was more reasonable than her sister and, in a thoroughly
English way, said that her subjects could believe what they liked so long as they outwardly

Temperature inversion over
Padley Manor in the Derwent
Valley in October

conformed to the Church of England. But, unfortunately for her (and her victims), there were many Catholics, known as 'recusants', to whom this compromise was totally unacceptable.

Elizabeth expressly singled out the Derbyshire Catholics as being 'backward and ill affected in religion'; and an agent reported that the High Peak 'where the papists have their harbours in the stony rocks' was 'a sanctuary for all wicked men'. Certainly the area around Hathersage remained a stronghold of both Catholicism and paganism (and indeed of that special brand of worship which was an amalgam of the two). May Games, with 'the nine worthies' and 'a goodly pageant', still coexisted quite happily with the 'pattering upon rosary beads' and 'other popish pedlary'. In particular, there was a cluster of recusants based around Padley Manor who would hide, as the circumstances demanded, in cleverly constructed 'hiding holes'. When Sir Thomas Fitzherbert was caught and imprisoned in 1561, his younger brother carried on with secret Masses despite frequent searches.

Meanwhile, the so-called 'Great Earl', the awful George Talbot, sixth Earl of Shrewsbury – who was now Bess of Hardwick's fourth husband – was keeping the Catholic Mary Queen of Scots (Elizabeth's cousin, and next in line to the throne) under house arrest at Chatsworth and other properties in and around the Peak. From Chatsworth, the ailing beauty made a number of trips to 'the baynes at Buckestones' to take the waters. After her first visit, she declared that she had 'not been at all disappointed, thank God'; but Elizabeth was furious, suspecting that she had been trying to escape. Mary protested 'before God' that she had no other object than her health.

But her friends had. Anthony Babington, a local man from Dethick who had been one of her pages in the early days of her captivity, planned to rescue her and assassinate Elizabeth. But the plot was rumbled, and Babington and thirteen others were brought to the scaffold in 1586. Babington pleaded with Elizabeth for his life, describing himself as a 'wretched synner with a pensive and contrite harte, most grivously bewaylinge his heynous trecherye' etc. But, as J B Firth has commented, he might as well have asked mercy of a stone as of Elizabeth. It was all to no avail, and Mary herself followed him to the scaffold the following year.

After these unfortunate events, the Great Earl – probably in an attempt to reinforce his Protestant credentials, especially in view of a new wave of anti-Catholicism now being directed at Spain – had a crackdown on the local recusants. On the very day that the Spanish Armada set sail in July 1588, he sallied forth into the Peak and raided Padley Hall. To his great satisfaction, two seminaries, Nicholas Garlick and Robert Ludlam, were discovered hiding in a chimney breast and were brought back to Derby, where they were hanged, drawn and quartered. Their sole crime – as Firth states drily – was that they were 'priests and, therefore, as a matter of course, false traitors to the Queen's most excellent majesty'.

Contemporaneous with the hardening of attitudes and increased Puritanism during Elizabeth's reign were important social changes that affected both the physical landscape and the fortunes of the poor. All through the sixteenth century, powerful landowners like the Talbots and the Cavendishes had been enclosing large areas of arable land for sheep grazing. The communal 'open fields' and large areas of common land which had been an essential part of the old system of subsistence farming were systematically walled in, bringing great hardship to the poorer yeomen. One spoke bitterly about landowners who 'live as though there were no God at all. They take our houses over our heads, they buy our grounds out of our hands, they raise our rents, they levy great (yea unreasonable) fines, they enclose our commons.' Another reflected sadly: 'How it will be good for the poor when the commons are taken away, I yet see not.'

As the landed gentry gained ever more wealth and power, the quality of life for the ordinary peasants declined. With neither the land to support them nor even, since the Dissolution of the Monasteries, religious almshouses to turn to, many became vagrants and beggars – only to be whipped for their sins, as was prescribed by harsh new laws. In the High Peak Hundred, 'rogues and vagabonds' who were able-bodied would be rounded up by parish constables and sent down the lead mines or, worse, find themselves pressed into military service (as happened in 1552 when more than 1,100 High Peak conscripts were assembled at Tideswell).

Labourers who were law-abiding were themselves little more than slaves. Magistrates in Quarter Session fixed both their hours of work and their wages, and anyone who disobeyed was liable to be fined £5 and serve a month in gaol. Craftsmen, such as carpenters, masons and bricklayers, received only a shilling a day, and tenpence a day in the winter. It is said that the men of Bradwell actually preferred to work in the lead mines, 'where they had their liberty rather than be under such servitude'.

In addition, all householders had to contribute four days a year to highway maintenance, and all tradesmen had to help with the harvest, or be punished by being put in the stocks. More serious misdemeanours would end at the gallows: for example, two men and a woman from the Peak were among a number of petty criminals publicly hanged at Derby gaol in 1578.

THE DEVIL'S OWN WORK

Hysterical bells of optimism rang out once again in the spring of 1603 to proclaim the coronation of James I. But the jubilation was sadly misplaced, for this brooding and uncommunicative man was obsessed with *'Daemonologie'*, on which he had written a lengthy treatise in 1597. The very first Bill of his first Parliament made witchcraft punishable by death on the first conviction. Renewed outbreaks of 'ye plague' – in Belper in 1603 and Ashbourne in 1605 – were now explained as the work of the devil, and thus of witches, who were his agent. Such was the fear the plague generated that anybody coming from these stricken villages, so obviously cursed, would be driven away with sticks and stones (as, indeed, they were at the later, more famous, Eyam plague of 1665). Before long, the fires of paranoia were being stoked with eyewitness accounts of 'devil gods' at witches' sabbaths wearing monstrous masks with candles spluttering between their horns. Anybody deemed to have the 'evil eye', like two Bakewell women in 1608, was likely to be burned alive as a witch; and an unfortunate spinster at Ilkeston met the same fate when she confessed under torture to having had 'unlawful dealings with the devil'.

The Derbyshire ram, or Tup, was now in the eyes of the Church the very embodiment of the devil; and Robin Hood, depicted as having ram's horns sprouting from his forehead, was branded 'the devil king of the fairy witch people'. Meanwhile, Hob, reduced to a 'hobgoblin', was, like Robin himself, associated with nothing so much as robbery. His 'houses' in Deep Dale, Monsal Dale and on East Moor above Chatsworth were also connected with fairies and elves, while the site of a prehistoric barrow south of Mam Tor became known as Elves' Hill (Eldon Hill). The 'bottomless' Eldon Hole was, like the Peakshole (Divillarse) at Castleton, the home of an ancient race of giants; and the 'high mountain' at Harboro became known as the 'Giant's Tomb'.

Nothing that was connected with the Old Religion was untainted: even the rowan tree was now commonly known as the 'Witch-Wiggin'; and the number nine, once the nine spheres of heaven had been conveniently forgotten and replaced by nine circles of hell, was regarded as particularly unlucky. The Nine Ladies on Stanton Moor had, according to the latest opinion, been turned into stone for their devilish practices, and the moon-goddess had been transmuted into the *'King's* Stone' to watch over them and see that they sinned no longer.

As for the Nine Stones at Nine Stones Close, the story got about that Robin Hood, in the form of a giant, had stood astride Hob's Hall with one foot on each of the pillars and urinated on to the meadow below – the very meadow where the Celtic settlement of Nine Stones Close had once stood. The nine virgins, witnessing this, had been so shocked that they were frozen to the spot and became nine old 'Grey Ladies' of stone – though some still claimed that on moonlit nights they might yet be seen spinning and cavorting to the sound of 'fairy pipes'.

Madness was in the air or, rather, the night sky – clearly situated in the bright, heathen disc of the moon; the vogue word on everybody's lips was suddenly *lunacy*.

In Monsal Dale below Hob's House, called in the time of the Stuarts 'Demon's Dale', adherents of the Old Religion would dance at the full moon wearing horns

Chatsworth in the time of Thomas Hobbes, which he described as 'the pleasantest lodging ever offered to the Muses'

Devonshire Collection, Chatsworth

HOBBES' HOUSE

It is the year 1640, and standing at the latticed windows of his study in Chatsworth Hall is the philosopher-in-residence, Thomas Hobbes. Now firmly ensconced in one of the grandest noble households in the land, this man of yeoman stock, with long hair and beady eyes, is staring far into space as if in a trance. Prescient, all-seeing.

For over an hour he has not moved, made no sound; and, being addicted to the new 'stinking combustible called tobacco', he is enveloped in a thick cloud of his own making. On his desk a battery of some half a dozen pipes lies in wait, already charged, like a row of cannons. But, as the haze around him thickens, so his mind clears. For not only can he hear, in his imagination, the moans and cries of the diseased and the oppressed beyond the outer wall of the garden – and behind it all, as a confused babble, the incomprehensible deprecations of the ecclesiastics – but he also has a clear vision of the horrors that are to come.

The madness and hatred that he can sense all around him, just beyond that outer wall – the almost palpable tension between Presbyterian and Catholic, king and commoner – can now lead to only one thing, which he dreads above all else: *Civil Warre.*

All the time he is composing his thoughts, hearing his own words resonating ever more loudly:

> ... and in this Darknesse of mind there ariseth such a Mist that they are made to fight one against another, without discerning their enemies from their friends ...

He makes a small gesture with his hand, scarcely a wave, to acknowledge his host and close friend, the young and handsome William Cavendish, the third Earl of Devonshire, coming through the garden gate with his younger brother Charles ...

> ... without a common Power to keep them all in awe, they are in that condition which is called Warre; and such a warre, as is of every man, against every man ... And from this proceed slaughter, solitude, and the want of all things ... no Arts; no Letters; no Society; and which is worst of all, continuall feare, and danger of violent death; And the life of man, solitary, poore, nasty, brutish, and short ...

Chatsworth Park today, seen from the slopes of the Rabbit Warren below Hob Hurst's House

Earlier in the day, in keeping with his standard routine of exercise in the morning and philosophical study in the afternoon, Hobbes had taken a long walk around the Chatsworth estate. Only today he had not stopped at the park wall but had gone striding all the way up to the brooding skyline of Harland Edge, and so out on to the wilds of East Moor. Although scathing about all forms of religious fanaticism, his obsession with his physical condition amounted almost to a religion in its own right. His fitness for a man of 52 was legendary; the earl once warned that 'he walks so fast up those hills that unless you are mounted on one of my ablest hunters you will not keep pace with him'. He was one of the first people on record to climb the Derbyshire hills simply for pleasure and exercise. This was indeed the only value a wild moorland like this had for him, for the 'state of nature' appalled him, and a landscape was increasingly 'frightful' to the extent that it lacked an obvious 'use'.

On the edge of East Moor he stopped briefly to look at the old prehistoric mound which the locals called 'Hob's House'. We need hardly guess what this clear-headed rationalist, who had studied the geometry of Euclid and met Galileo in Italy, thought of it. For he rejected all 'superstitions', pagan and Christian alike, as 'phantasms of the braine'. Elves and goblins, 'the soul', 'transubstantiation', 'holy water' and even 'good luck' were all equally absurd. The daringly outspoken, often outrageous Hobbes had no time for Hob or any of the other pagan gods. They were nothing more than 'the Fancies of ignorant people, rising from the Traditions of old Wives'.

THE GREAT LEVIATHAN

In place of any kind of supernatural being, Hobbes had advocated a *mortal* god, or a 'Great Leviathan' – a supreme ruler to 'keep them all in awe' and prevent them from falling into civil war and anarchy. But when this Great Leviathan materialized in the form of the 'Long Parliament' in the autumn of 1640, and a direct conflict with the king became inevitable, Hobbes 'went over into France – the first of all that fled', as he later admitted.

Yet again in its history, the Peak was in a strategic position of central importance, being the chief physical barrier between the two main Royalist strongholds of the south Midlands and Yorkshire. And once again the lead mines had an important part to play, this time in the manufacture of gunmetal and bullets; and there was the additional asset of the lead miners themselves, with their legendary toughness and special trenching skills.

The nobility, who – with the exception of the Earl of Rutland (the owner of Haddon Hall) – were Royalist to a man, showed a remarkable reluctance to get involved and did little to raise troops for the king. Their support, when it came, was a classic case of too little, too late, and by Christmas 1642 the whole of Derbyshire had fallen under the control of the loathsome and malicious Sir John Gell of Hopton, who was with justification likened by his enemies to the devil.

The experience of the Presbyterian Rector of Ashover, who had resolved to remain neutral, was typical of many:

> The next daye a companie of dragoones came to the hall and demanded possession in the name of the High Court of Parliament, which I at once did give, but I told them that I had done nothing against the Parliament; but they replied with all civility that they had orders from their commanding officer to destroy the hall. They, however, offered to assist me in removing anything I set store bye.

Once they had blown up the hall and left it in ruins, they sang a psalm. Then they

> marched to the church, and for fear they should injure the house of God, I did soon follow after, and to my great surprise did find the scout-master Smedley in the pulpit, when he did preach a sermon two hours long about Popery, Priestcraft and Kingcraft; but Lord! what stuff and nonsense he did talke, and if he could have murdered the Kyng as easily as he did the Kyng's English, the war would long since have been over.

Late in the following year (1643), Charles Cavendish, who had distinguished himself in the cavalry charge with Prince Rupert at Edgehill, was killed at Gainsborough. But soon afterwards the Royalist forces under his uncle, the Marquis of Newcastle, re-entered Derbyshire via Chesterfield, 'like demons destroying all'. Having retaken Wingfield Manor and Bakewell, they pushed on towards Staffordshire. At Hartington, where six and sixteen centuries earlier the limestone hills had echoed with the sounds of slaughter, there was again carnage when the Royalists overran the enemy garrison and chased the fleeing survivors 'near five miles together (almost to Leek), doing sharp execution all the way'. However, developments in the north prevented the Marquis of Newcastle from exploiting this advance, and the remaining Royalists were soon repulsed and then cut to pieces by Colonel Gell's forces at Wirksworth. Had Newcastle remained in the

Peak and breached the enemy-held corridor across the Midlands, who knows what *might* have happened?

Although the war dragged on for another four years, the Royalist cause was effectively lost at Naseby in the following year. But the turmoil for the local villagers did not end, for it was in this very period, in which the Puritan extremists tightened their grip on the whole fabric of English life, that witch-hunting reached its most ferocious climax. The self-styled 'Witchfinder-General', Matthew Hopkins, indulged in varieties of sadism – such as 'pricking', ducking and blood-letting – which are too frightful to recount in detail.

It is thought that about 2,000 men lost their lives in Derbyshire in the Civil War, out of a population of 60,000, but many more were maimed for life. Most of the powerful landowning families suffered losses (as well as being financially ruined by the Sequestration Committee). The Earl of Devonshire, who had joined Hobbes in exile in France in 1642, mourned the loss of his brother, Charles Cavendish; the Earl of Chesterfield, the loss of two sons; and Colonel Thomas Eyre, who had fought in a hand-to-hand encounter with Cromwell at Edgehill, died of wounds and neglect in Derby gaol.

In the period that followed the execution of Charles I in January 1649 – called with calculated perversity the 'Commonwealth' (the very term that Hobbes had given to his ideal society) – England became a military state run by Major-Generals under the ruthless hand of the 'Lord Protector', Oliver Cromwell. In the chilling belief that God was on his side, and that 'the Word and the Sword must be joined', Cromwell pursued his mission with, as Brian Stone has put it, 'a single-minded tenacity rivalled, in our day, only by the dogmatism of the Marxist or the fanaticism of the Nazi'. Scarcely a single traditional pleasure was permitted: gaming with cards, dancing around the maypole, travelling on a Sunday – even celebrating Christmas – all were banned in the name of 'godliness and virtue'. Alehouses were closed as 'nests of Satan', and regular fasts were held in the Peak on the second Thursday of each month.

Unsurprisingly, despite the operations of Cromwell's secret service, there was seething unrest. A group of Royalists, now with much Presbyterian support, met in Sherwood Forest in the summer of 1659 and did battle with the local militia. Retreating in disarray, some fled to Derby where, to uproar, a 'Declaration in favour of the King' was read in the market-place, with 'some crying a King, others a Free Parliament, some both', before troops brought the disturbance under control.

THE GREEN MAN IS BACK

The Royalists did not have long to wait. Only nine months later, in May 1660, news reached the Peak that Charles II had landed in Dover with the intention of restoring 'the whole nation to its primitive temper and integrity, to its good old manners, its good old humour and its good old nature'; and when he was proclaimed king in Derby market-place, the sound of rejoicing rang out from the church tower of All Saints and swept across the county in a great mellifluence of pealing bells.

All over the Peak, the old spring festivals were quickly revised as a 'thanksgiving day for restoringe a Kinge'. At Ilkeston, on the day the king arrived in London (29 May) a great pyramid of oak boughs was erected around an old standing stone, and at its summit the traditional 'mother-goddess' was replaced by a waxen figure called 'Charles of the Oak'. And at Castleton on the same day – which they called Oak Apple Day – the church tower was adorned with branches of oak, elm and sycamore, and the Green Man, now called the 'king' but still wearing a green costume and with an enormous garland of flowers over his head like an oversized hood, led the procession around the village on horseback.

The Green Man was back, but with much of his significance lost. Robin, the Lord of Misrule, had been transformed into the faintly amusing 'Robin Goodfellow'. The king and Robin had become one, with their original powers heavily curtailed.

But there was a new atmosphere of religious toleration. The Peak remained a place for dissenters, and for not playing by the rules. Clandestine services in the 'old Puritan style' were held by Nonconformist Protestants at Alport Castles Farm in one of the remotest parts of the Peak; and from 1665, when the parson was given powers to grant marriage licences without banns, Peak Forest became a sort of Gretna Green of the Peak for eloping couples.

Perhaps we can judge with hindsight that, in the High Peak at least, although it had been tried to extremes, the old Celtic balance had never been completely lost. Now everything had come round full circle, as the villagers once again danced around their maypoles, as they had danced around their stone circles of old. And at Tideswell, Burbage and Wirksworth, in a ceremony known as 'clipping', the parishioners pranced around their churches, all holding hands, like an oversized version of ring-o'-roses.

After the long hard 'winter' and 'silent Christmases' of Cromwell's Commonwealth, the air in the spring of 1660 was full of the sound of bells and singing, with the spirit of the new age being expressed in the words of a 'carol' at Castleton:

> Our Saviour arose, our own Heaven's King,
> The sun and the moon did both rise with Him,
> And was this not a joyful thing?...

After the bloodied pendulum, an ecstatic whirl of new optimism, gathering momentum with the ever faster revolution of scientific and democratic 'progress'. The sound of singing soon blends with the sound of wheels, new wheels turning.

We can hear them now ...

6 Arcadia in the wilderness

We move forward sixty years, to the sound of a new kind of wheels and a new kind of music: faster, smoother-running, more confident wheels, turning with all the precision of Bach's 'Well-tempered Clavier', published in this very year of 1722.

... And, at this start of all modern music, we find ourselves in a new age in which everything has changed. In our sixty-year carriage-ride into the future, there has been a truly Glorious Revolution in which Natural Philosophy has come 'in with a spring-tide' and 'all the old Rubbish' has been thrown away. The absolute separation of Church and State that Hobbes demanded has come to pass; England has its first Prime Minister (Robert Walpole) and its first regularly elected Parliament; and in place of 'lunacy', the word now on everyone's lips is 'toleration' (freedom of worship being granted to all dissenters – but still not to Catholics). The 'incomparable Mr Newton' has discovered the laws of gravity and motion; the Royal Society has been formed to 'promote the welfare of the arts and sciences'; Newcomen has invented the first practical steam engine; that 'great engine of State', the Bank of England, has been founded; and the singular entity, 'Great Britain', has been born out of the 'perfect union' of England and Scotland.

And, as we draw closer, on this very road out of Derby where at another turning point in history outsiders had come on chariots, we find ourselves looking at one particular coach and horses, which contains another outsider of sorts. Coming closer still we can hear the sounds of animated conversation. Actually, it is more of a monologue, since most of the talking is coming from one extraordinary 62-year-old man, who at different stages in his life has adopted many guises: a would-be Presbyterian minister, a wealthy businessman, a bankrupt, an economic theorist, a ship insurer, a parapsychologist, a demonic fantasist, a criminal biographer, a political prisoner, a champion of moderation and democracy, an activist in the Duke of Monmouth's rebellion, a secret agent for the Whigs, a secret agent for the Tories, a writer of ghost stories and a political satirist. Today, this shape-shifter of the new age is better known as the most prolific writer in the English language and 'the father of the English novel', the author of *Robinson Crusoe* – Mr Daniel Defoe. Having just completed *Moll Flanders* and *A Journal of the Plague Year* he is taking a break from writing, and although his imagination is still running wild on more fanciful journeys – trips around the world, or even to the moon – what he is engaged on now is a 'Tour through the Whole Island of Great Britain'.

As one of the first great travelling writers – before Pennant, Johnson and Boswell – and one who is well attuned to the brave new world of market economics and scientific progress, Defoe is the perfect mirror and representative of the age. Today he has already

We advanced due north, and, mounting the hills gradually for four or five miles, we soon had a most frightful view indeed among the black mountains of the Peak

Daniel Defoe

I took with me a Gentleman of my Acquaintance who was a walking library and a moveable map

been holding forth on his 'beloved subject', the importance of trade – how it 'raises new species of Wealth, which Nature knew nothing of', and has 'two daughters – namely Manufacture and Navigation'; and, talking of navigation, he is also a great enthusiast for the new turnpike roads, which in the last year or two have made 'wonderful improvements' to travel. And now he is saying, with a touch of irony, as they bounce along the very rough and rutted Old Portway towards Wirksworth, that within a few years he expects to see most of the roads in England 'restored to the same good condition that they were in during the Roman government ...'

Sadly, they had to leave these wonderful new roads behind a few days ago when they crossed the Trent – Defoe called it 'crossing the Rubicon'. But now he is bubbling over with a new excitement, scarce knowing 'which way to set forward, in a country so full of wonders'. He has always wanted to visit the Peak, ever since reading Hobbes' famously terse list of its 'Seven Wonders' – *Aedes, Mons, Barathrum, binus Fons, Antraque bina* (a house, a mountain, a chasm, two fountains and two caves) – and, later, an evocative account by Celia Fiennes, the adventurous daughter of one of Cromwell's officers who rode side-saddle through the Peak in 1697. 'All Darbyshire', she reported, 'is but a world of peaked hills as thick as can be – so full of moore or quagmires and such precipices that one that is a stranger cannot travell without a Guide.' Now Defoe was finding out what she meant.

What seems like many hours ago, they left Derby, and now they are holding tight to their handstraps as they bounce along the 'base, stony, and mountainous' track over Wirksworth Moor to Matlock with 'a most frightful view indeed among the black mountains of the Peak, as yet at a distance'. Defoe's companion, a gentleman he has

brought with him who is 'a walking library and a moveable map', is feeling sick; but all the father of the modern novel can say is, 'By heavens! it's not as injurious as being in the pillory, or being imprisoned at Newgate' (both of which he's experienced).

At last, with the carriage bouncing and squeaking cantankerously on its C-springs, they reach a boggy track beside 'that fury of a river called the Derwent' ('a frightful creature when the hills load her current with water'), and here they come across their first great wonder ...

▶ The River Derwent with High Tor in the background

On the east side of the Derwent stands a high rock, which rises from the very bottom of the river. I say, it rises perpendicular as a wall, the precipice bare and smooth like one plain stone, to such a prodigious height, it is really surprising ... I looked upon it very curiously, for they told me it was above four hundred foot high, which is as high as two of our Monuments, one set upon another. The prodigious height of this tor was to me more a wonder than any of the rest in the Peak, and, I think, should be named among them.

Daniel Defoe, *A Tour through the Whole Island of Great Britain,* 1726

▶ High Tor in late November

... And now the rocking, creaking, juddering carriage is struggling up on to 'a vast extended moor or waste, which presents you with neither hedge, house or tree, but a waste and howling wilderness', and there is the smell of heather and grass and wide open spaces. Then, just before reaching the little hamlet of Robin Hood, they branch left on an even wilder track across that 'comfortless and barren' part of East Moor which has recently become known as Gibbet Moor – for it is here that, scarcely twenty years before, the last live gibbeting in England took place.

On Beeley Moor

Defoe is no doubt oblivious of this for he is still talking profusely. Today the conversation has ranged all the way from the history of the union of Great Britain to the history of the devil, from Turkish spies and the czars of Muscovy to pirates, street-walkers and beautiful women; and now he is talking so much (he's pretending to be a priest pontificating about *the shortest way of dealing with dissenters*) that he does not notice the ancient burial mound of Hob's House slipping past them on the right, nor, a little later, a 60-foot stone circle, half-hidden in the heather. It's a wonder, with all this talking, that he notices anything at all.

Nothing can be more surprising of its kind, than for a stranger wandering or labouring to pass this difficult desert country, and seeing no end of it, and almost discouraged and beaten out with the fatigue of it, (just such was our case) when on a sudden the guide brings him to this precipice, where he looks down from a frightful height ...

... into the most delightful valley, with the most pleasant garden, and most beautiful palace in the world. If there is any wonder in Chatsworth, it is that any man who had a genius suitable to so magnificent a design, who could lay out the plan for such a house, would build it in such a situation, and in such a country so out of the way, so concealed from the world.

Daniel Defoe, *A Tour through the Whole Island of Great Britain*

THE MOST BEAUTIFUL PALACE IN THE WORLD

The great 'Palace of the Peak', the Chatsworth that we know today, was only fifteen years old when Defoe saw it in 1722. The man who 'had the genius suitable to so magnificent a design' was the fourth Earl of Devonshire, who had been one of the 'immortal seven' signatories responsible for the 'Glorious Revolution' of 1688 which had ousted the Catholic James II in favour of his Protestant daughter Mary and her Dutch husband, Prince William of Orange, who was called by Defoe 'the Glorious, Great, and Good, and Kind'.

As a reward, William of Orange had given the earl first, in 1690, the whole of the High Peak Hundred, previously the Royal Forest of the Peak, including all the lead-mining rights around Castleton, and then, in 1694, he had made him the first Duke of Devonshire. Now one of the most powerful people in the land after the monarch, all that was left for him to do was build a suitably regal palace to go with his role of Lord Lieutenant of Derbyshire and Steward of the High Peak.

The philosopher of the age, John Locke, who wrote extensively on the subject of private property, said that a person had exclusive rights to any particular part of the earth only to the extent that he improved it. Well, the Duke of Devonshire had certainly done that. Working closely with the architect William Talman, he had created a vast edifice of opulent splendour which was at once a statement of balanced proportion, power and enshrined privilege, and an epitome of all that the Glorious Revolution and the new 'Augustan Age' stood for.

FROM ANCIENT GREENWOOD TO PARADISE GARDEN

But building an enormous country palace was only the beginning of the duke's project. In keeping with the latest fashion, he next created an impressive garden – laid out in the formal 'French style' on geometrical principles that Hobbes would surely have approved of – and then a vast open park around it. 'Down with the oaks from the front and wings is the modern cry,' said one commentator in 1763, and a poet spoke of the landowner's need to 'cut down ev'ry Tree / That clouded th'ambitious prospect of his eye'.

There was a hidden agenda to all this intensive tree-felling. First, there was the perception that it was 'unhealthful to live near a wood', for its dark recesses were, after all, the last refuge of paganism. It was vitally necessary to strip away the mysteries of the 'plebeian underwood' – as one poet actually called it – since it was still dimly remembered as a rival 'seat' of power. But secondly, and more importantly, deforesting had become an economic necessity, for there was an enormous new demand for wood, not just for iron and lead smelting but overwhelmingly now for shipbuilding: a single man-of-war or a mercantile 'East Indiaman', for example, would consume well over a thousand mature oaks apiece.

The nobility's woodland had assumed a position of the greatest importance, for all other forests were already seriously depleted. The abolition of the Royal Forests during the Civil Wars had led to a state of anarchy in which great armies of common people had, in the words of Simon Schama, 'whacked and hacked at anything they could find'; and Charles II's aggressive naval and colonising policies had led to a further level of depredation. Now the Whig oligarchy, heavily involved in furthering wars against the French and Spanish, had become, in effect, the protectors and suppliers of timber to the navy.

Any archaic greenwood scruples were easily overcome in economic and nationalistic terms. British woodland was a symbol of maritime strength, and much nonsense was talked about the 'national character of a British ship' and the British oak being superior to that of other nations. Like many of his contemporaries, Defoe was an ardent supporter of this shipbuilding programme and demanded that 'ancient oaks' with 'their withered tops' be 'cut down and made serviceable to their country'. Once wood had acquired such a *commercial* value, who heeded the old Celtic injunction against cutting down oaks, whether living or dead? Parliamentary statutes, not ancient taboos, were the way forward in this new, progressive, utilitarian age. In a ghostly, ghastly reincarnation of the Forest Law of 600 years before (with its 'transgressions against the verte') a 'Black Act' of 1722 made it a capital offence for tenants to cut down trees. Harsh enforcement of the law was also a way in which selfish landlords could limit the supply of oaks to force up prices, to the extent that some even accused them of being irresponsible and unpatriotic.

Having created broad vistas – to help build up the navy and keep back the locals – the propertied aristocracy turned their attention to the environment itself. This was a very new form of possession which involved an extreme, idealized vision of how the whole palace domain should look. The magnate now was God, who could move mountains, or at least whole hills and villages if he so wished. Where previously it had sufficed to keep the plebs at bay, now they had to be eradicated from view. The fourth Duke of Devonshire, who was already known as the 'Crown Prince of the Whigs' for his regal and domineering manner, demolished that part of medieval Edensor which could be seen from the house.

No! those days are gone away,
And their hours are old and gray ...
No, the bugle sounds no more,
And the twanging bow no more...
Gone, the tough-belted outlaw,
Idling in the "grene shaw";
All are gone away and past!
And if Robin should be cast
Sudden from his turfed grave ...
He would swear, for all his oaks,
Fall'n beneath the dockyard strokes,
Have rotted on the briny seas ...

John Keats, 1818

Before and after in Chatsworth Park

His accomplice in these and other changes in 1761-2 was one Lancelot Brown, the leading 'improver of grounds' in the country, better known as 'Capability' Brown from his disturbing habit of saying that a landscape had 'capabilities'. For him, raw nature did no more than provide the basic ingredients of a landscape; his calling in life was the tidying up or, as he termed it, the 'dressing' of nature on a massive scale. At Chatsworth, in keeping with the latest fashion – which conveniently coincided with both a contemporary movement for 'patriotic planting' and yet another timber-crunching war against the French – Capability cleverly combined a programme of felling with one of planting. In place of the earlier formal plantations he created a park with a natural, unplanned appearance, planting trees in clumps or loose belts which carefully avoided any obvious symmetry. But, for all its feigned naturalism, this enclosed park was, of course, utterly at odds with the wild old Derwent Forest which it replaced.

This new, 'informal' parkland had extended the idea of a country seat to appropriate the whole landscape around it; and at its centre was a house more detached from its surroundings than any Peakland home had ever been before – a distant chimera of a palace set in a vast Paradise Garden from which all elements of common society were excluded and kept unseen beyond the surrounding hills.

Capability Brown's park around Chatsworth. When Defoe saw it, forty years before Brown had gone to work, the house was surrounded by formal gardens laid out in the 'Grand French' style, expressing a sense of military might

OUTSIDE THE PARADISE GARDEN

Outside the robust gritstone walls of the Chatsworth estate lay a very different world, shockingly at variance with the Whigs' rosy-spectacled view of progress, in which there had been an appalling increase in poverty, largely as a result of the enclosure of open fields and the final extinction of common-use rights.

The Puritans may technically have been defeated at the Restoration but Puritanism as an attitude of mind was alive and well. As the wealth of the privileged had increased, so their charity had contracted. Beggars were described as 'insolente and threatteninge' and market-day floggings were still a common spectacle. Undernourished rustics who had traditionally relied on poaching were referred to in the 'Black Act' of 1722 as

'wicked and evil-disposed persons', and the Draconian new penalties that were levelled against them created a whole new generation of outlaws. The woods and moorland around the eastern edges were once again, as of old, full of armed robbers, while in the towns mob violence became commonplace. Such disturbances were suppressed by the militia, and hangings and transportations invariably followed. All the time, the laws dealing with crimes against property were strengthened so that, incredibly, by 1740 children could be hanged for stealing a handkerchief.

Perhaps the most haunting reminder of the unacceptable face of the new 'Augustan Age' is the tale of how Gibbet Moor received its name. In the time that the first Duke of Devonshire's palace was nearing completion, a tramp who had killed a woman for refusing him food – he poured the boiling fat from her frying pan down her throat – was sentenced to be hanged alive in chains by her cottage door, scarcely a mile from the estate wall. He took a long time to die, and it is said that his screams were so piercing as he swung on his gibbet that they could be heard by the duke in his palace, shattering his Arcadian idyll.

Just as the Derwent Forest had been emaciated and tamed, so the oaken-hearted people of the Peak were subdued. As the sacred grove went to the sawmill, so the vestiges of old pagan customs were reduced to quaint antiquarian diversions which they were not meant to understand but vaguely to enjoy. The old custom – at Hallowe'en, Christmas or Plough Monday – of 'guising' (meaning to dress or disguise: all that now remained of Celtic shape-shifting) had been reduced to a dumb show in which a 'mummer' in fancy dress acted out a foolish ceremonial. Typically, he would be wearing a sheepskin and horns to represent 'Old Tup', the Ram, and would be 'sacrificed' by having his throat 'cut'.

Thus were the old gods reduced to objects of ridicule. Hob became 'Hob i' th' Hurst', a temperamental elf who lurked in the forests and around burial mounds and would appear at May Day as the 'hobbyhorse' (which in some villages was actually called 'Old Hob'). Robin Hood himself was now no more than the May Bride's lover – the May Bride, Maid Marian, being a comparatively recent addition to the myth. And, most risible of all, the Green Man would make his appearance as 'Jack-in-the-Green', now nothing more than an object of amusement at a freak show.

The maypole on the green, beribboned and prettified, had become simply an emblem of rural happiness tinged with national pride. At news of victory over the Spanish in 1711, the Duke of Devonshire saw to it that the occasion was marked by joyous dancing around the maypole accompanied by the inevitable bell-ringing – as if the Peak people were really interested in these distant wars, except in so far as they wrested young men from their homes (as had happened in Youlgreave in 1710, when three men were seized by constables in a violent scuffle).

Just as the ancient barrows were now identified with 'fairy mounds', so the ancient lead-mining People of the Peak, the Pecsaetna, had been reduced to 'Peakrills', the very name carrying overtones of 'little people' – elves or hobgoblins whose natural habitat lay far underground. And yet, as Daniel Defoe grasped full well when he met the lead miners of Brassington in 1722, they were not to be underestimated. Indeed, it was his final judgement that they were 'the greatest of all the wonders of the Peak, for they are bold, daring, even desperate kind of fellows in their search into the bowels of the earth; for no people in the world out-do them'.

Could *anything* outdo these rock-hardened people now?

7 Satanic mills

Speaking as a tourist, these vales have lost all their beauties.—Every rural sound is sunk in the
clamours of cotton works; and the simple peasant is changed into the impudent mechanic:—
the woods find their way into the canals; and the rocks are disfigured for lime stone. The vales
are every way block'd up by mills.

The Hon. John Byng describing the Cromford area in June 1790

HIDDEN RICHES

The magic, life-giving power of the rock, and of the water flowing through it, which we
have touched on frequently in this brief survey of the Peak's history, was at last seen in
purely economic terms in the early years of the Hanoverians. The only value that the
landscape now had was as a potential source of wealth. In the more Puritan age in
which Celia Fiennes had lived, the fact that these barren-looking hills were 'impregnated
with rich Marbles Stones Metals Iron and Copper and Coale mines in their bowells'
had seemed to her to be an act of God; while, in the Enlightenment that followed,
Daniel Defoe had put a more businesslike slant on it, stating that, in 'this otherwise
frightful country', the abundance of riches seemed to have been 'directed by the wise
hand of Providence for manufactures'.

The extraordinarily difficult terrain of the Peak, and the 'frightful creature' of the
Derwent, which hitherto had been nothing but an obstacle, suddenly had a pivotal role
in providing the power and minerals for the economic and scientific revolution which
was now taking place. Once they had their 'fire-engines' – as Newcomen's steam engines
were commonly called – the lead miners could pump the dangerous floodwaters from
their mines and delve ever deeper into the earth. The soughers who made the necessary
drainage channels tunnelled like moles through the bare rock, armed only with picks
and wedges, at the rate of three-quarters of an inch an hour, a quarter of a mile a
decade.

The new industries fed off one another in an ever-expanding circle of dependence.
The steam engines required coal, iron and brass, which in turn required copper. The
coal came from Codnor by canal; the iron from blast furnaces at Alderwasley – which
in turn obtained limestone for flux from the nearby quarry at Crich; and the copper
came from enormous mines at Ecton Hill, owned by the Duke of Devonshire, which
were among the richest in Britain. One particularly monstrous cavern, reached by a
shaft 1,300 feet deep, was described by William Efford in 1769 as 'a place as horrible to
view as imagination can conceive. On the passage down, the constant blasting of the
rocks, ten times louder than the loudest thunder, seems to roll and shake the whole
body of the mountain.'

◀ Weir in Monsal Dale below
Hob's House

THE GREATER FELON

The law doth punish man or woman
That steals the goose from off the common,
But lets the greater felon loose,
That steals the common from the goose.

Anonymous, late eighteenth century

Meanwhile, in the wilder parts of the Peak the enclosure of common lands was continuing apace; indeed, in the reign of George III (1760–1820) it reached its height, with dozens of private Enclosure Acts being brought before Parliament by local landlords. At Brassington, for example, despite their earlier 'warmest opposition' to any such suggestion by local landowners like the Gells, the people lost their commons with a 'successful' Enclosure Act of 1803 and the 'award' five years later. The abuse of the English language involved here was as nothing compared with the abuse of the people. Most of the land was 'awarded' to a few landowners who lived outside the district, while the lords and ladies of the manor themselves received only *one-eighteenth* of the remainder.

So it was that the independent class of yeoman freeholder on the edge of the common vanished for ever. 'Cut down', as the poet Southey put it in 1816, 'with as little remorse and as little discrimination as old timber', he was left with just a cottage garden and minimal compensation. Reduced to being a mere labourer for a big farmer, he was told that enclosure was essential for 'the good of the nation', for this was the only way to increase corn production and so win the economic struggle with Napoleon. The truth was a lot simpler: enclosure was a means of keeping the people in their place, as a report to the Board of Agriculture in 1794 had stated unequivocally: 'the subordination of the lower ranks of society, which in the present times is much wanted, would be hereby considerably secured'.

'The English farmer', William Cobbett wrote in 1816, 'has, of late years, become a totally different character. A fox-hunting horse; polished boots; a spanking trot to market; a "get out of the way or by G–d I'll ride over you" to every poor devil upon the road; wine at his dinner; a servant to wait at his table; a painted lady for a wife; sons aping the young squires and lords; a house crammed up with sofas, pianos, and all sorts of fooleries.' His real objection, though, was that 'when farmers become gentlemen, their labourers become slaves', for their vast new mansions were paid for by ever larger rents. Even Arthur Young, who had been the chief architect of enclosure in the 1780s, admitted by 1801 that 'By nineteen out of twenty Enclosure Bills the poor are injured and most grossly'.

Once again, as in days of old, hardship, poverty and exclusion drove the people to poaching in spite of penalties so severe that Henry II would have been proud of them. By 1820, transportation – the most widely used means of getting rid of Malthus's 'surplus population' – was the penalty even for carrying a net. But, as in the dark days of Robin Hood, the dangerous 'sport' of poaching was accepted by the majority of Peak people as both moral and necessary. In the words of the historian G M Trevelyan, it 'brought a gleam of romance and joyous living into the life of the disinherited peasant. The woods at midnight resounded with volleys when gentlemen and their servants, in parties of a dozen or twenty, were grappling with the banditti, man to man.'

Icy wall on windswept Rowlee
Pasture, near Alport Castles,
after a night of freezing rain

THE DEVIL TUNES HIS BAGPIPES

As the cottage-based textile industry was displaced by machines, so life in the country
became ever more wretched. But in one area of the Peak the people were lucky. In 1771
a semi-literate one-time barber and wig-maker by the name of Richard Arkwright arrived
at the 'remote' and relatively inaccessible hamlet of Scarthin close to the important
Cromford river-crossing of the Derwent. He also happened to be a mechanical genius,
and was looking for a secluded location in which to develop his highly secret new
roller-spinning frame, away from the hostility of the Nottingham handspinners. Also,
while his first spinning frames had been horse powered, he was now looking for a
cheaper and more efficient form of power.

The swift Bonsall brook, which already provided power for the corn and lead-smelting
mills at Scarthin, was a good starting point, but Arkwright cleverly supplemented it
with the much more substantial outfall of Cromford Sough, the underground tunnel
which drained the Wirksworth lead field. Apart from the considerable power it provided,
the water from the sough had a less obvious advantage: coming from deep underground,
it never froze, even in the hardest winter. The Cromford site was clever for a further
reason: the lead-mining industry was in decline, which meant that Arkwright had a
plentiful supply of cheap labour. The lucky few involved with his new spinning frame,
powered by a ten-horsepower waterwheel, had never seen anything like it, while
passers-by compared the strange noises it produced with 'the devil tuning his bagpipes'.

Arkwright's first cotton mill was such a success that he rapidly expanded his operation,
building two more at Cromford, and others at Bakewell and Cressbrook in the Wye
Valley – so that, by the time of the storming of the Bastille in 1789, he had created a

revolution all of his own. His 'factory village' at Cromford employed over a thousand people working on the first real 'production line' in Britain, with the additional benefits of decent accommodation, a Sunday school, and a system of rewards as incentives. 'There is so much water, so much rock, so much population and so much wood', a distinguished visitor exclaimed in 1790, 'that it looks like a Chinese town!'

Although Arkwright was an arrogant man, who was described by his enemies as a tyrant, in the context of the times he was a benevolent visionary. Unquestionably a hard taskmaster, he represented a new breed of industrial patriarch, almost the equivalent of a feudal lord, complete with his own castle which he had built across the river at Willersley (but did not live long enough to use). By the time of his death in 1792 he was the High Sheriff of the county, a millionaire and had been knighted by George III.

By the turn of the century similar, grim, fortress-like cotton mills had sprung up all along the Derwent – all the way from Darley Abbey and Belper to such far-flung sites as Bamford and Edale. They had a major impact on the landscape. A few lone critics, such as Uvedale Price, were appalled. 'Nothing can equal them', he said in 1810, 'for the purpose of disbeautifying an enchanting piece of scenery.' But most of his contemporaries waxed lyrical, seeing in them everything that was most romantic. 'These cotton mills, seven stories high, and fill'd with inhabitants', reminded John Byng of 'a first rate man of war; and when they are lighted up, on a dark night, they look most luminously beautiful.' Cressbrook Mill, in particular, captivated people. William Adam marvelled at such 'a wonderful structure in such a position, for we seem here shut in on all sides, apparently *far, very far* from the great world. It is indeed a romantic spot.' Mary Sterndale went further, calling it 'this glory of a commercial nation', an 'illumined palace raised by the power of magic'. And more wonderful still, this enchanting place was run by a poet – the so-called 'Minstrel of the Peak', William Newton, who taught his apprentices music, so that 'the hallelujahs of Handel fill the valley'.

To gauge just how enchanting this 'illumined palace' really was, we need perhaps to take a step closer.

◀ Litton Mill today

HALLELUJAH!

> We talk of our commercial greatness – of the importance of manufactures, and the advantages
> thereby conferred upon the country; but most of us little know what all this means, and is; how
> it has been brought about; and what it has done, and is now doing.
>
> Joseph Rayner Stephens, a Chartist clergyman, writing of Cressbrook Mill in 1849

What are these raucous sounds we have been told are hallelujahs?... They are children's voices all right, but this awful high-pitched wailing is altogether less like a jubilate of Handel than a threnody for lost souls.

When we enter these long-forgotten windows and open the history books, all we can hear are the sounds of pain and fear. The Reverend Joseph Rayner Stephens speaks in horror of a form of slavery which existed here at the beginning of the nineteenth century – in 'this boasted land of freedom' – which was 'as revolting and diabolical' as any that had ever existed 'on the coast of Africa. Thousands upon thousands of fatherless and friendless children have been bought and sold ...'

The testimony which this shocked clergyman amassed in 1849 (which only re-emerged in 1980) has done little so far to shake the long-established view that, in sharp distinction to the notorious Ellis Needham of Litton Mill just a mile and a half upstream, William Newton of Cressbrook was 'ahead of his time in his treatment of apprentices'. Recent research has shown that the conditions in both mills was in fact very similar.

Peel's Health and Morals of Apprentices Act of 1802, which required all mills to be regularly inspected, was as ineffective as its title was pretentious, as was an Act of 1816 which set a limit of forty miles to the distance from which children could be obtained. The 'Minstrel of the Peak', William Newton, got round this quite simply by procuring his children through Royal Military Asylums which, not being parish workhouses, were outside the scope of the Act. In this way he could obtain nine-year old children from as far away as London and Southampton.

One ten-year-old boy from Bethnal Green related many years later how he had been asked whether he would like to go into the country; he was told that he had grown a fine lad and would soon become a man and earn his twenty shillings a week. He was also told what sport he would have among the hills, 'catching hares and rabbits, and fishing in the brooks and streams'.

On his arrival at Cressbrook in January 1820 this London lad found himself 'number 253' of four hundred. The boys slept six to a bed – each 'bed' being 'something like a cart frame or a packing case filled with straw. When they changed the straw, it was just the same as tossing straw up for horses.'

The Bethnal Green 'prentices worked for a year in the clothes they had arrived in. Soon they 'were nearly naked, without shoes or stockings'. Work started at six in the morning and continued non-stop, apart from a half-hour lunch break, until nine or ten at night. Breakfast was eaten as best they could, the wheel never stopping. 'Every night when we got our suppers we sat round the table, and prayers were read to us out of the common prayer book. A man walked up and down between the tables with a stick to keep us from going to sleep. We finished by singing a psalm.' Was this perhaps when they broke out into their joyous hallelujahs? 'We never tasted flour bread, except once a year, Christmas Eve, when we had what we called a flour cake dry without butter.'

Apart from terrible injuries from the machines, with arms regularly being mangled, grievous bodily harm was inflicted by all kinds of sadistic punishments. When the

London boys, who had been told they would have great 'sport' in the country, went bird-nesting in the woods and Newton spotted them, 'he ordered the watchman to strip us, made us mount on one another's backs, and would himself flog us with these hazel sticks across our bare buttocks till he made the blood flow. I was stiff and bloody for weeks and could hardly walk. I had nothing to put on it but factory oil to keep it moist. My shirt and trowsers kept sticking to it.'

The girls were treated equally badly. The normal punishment for talking to a boy was to have their hair cut off with a carving knife. And, like the boys, they endured frequent beatings. Once, when a girl called Mary spilled some slops on the floor, 'Mr Newton kicked her where he should not do, and a heavy sleepiness came over her, and she wore away and died'.

Perhaps the saddest case of all was that of Betsy Witnough. For throwing away and not eating some bad bread

> Mr Newton beat her till she could not see out of her eyes, they were so swelled up. One day Betsy crept out unknown to them to get some water. She was so dry she could abide no longer. They went out to seek her and found her in the fish pond. Everything was done by her to bring her about. But she was dead enough.

This was no doubt the 'beautiful lake' described by Adam. What a romantic spot it was! And so far, so 'very far from the great world'...

◄ A jolly spot. The 'beautiful lake' and weir at Cressbrook Mill, Water-cum-Jolly

HARD TIMES

For the adult workers in the new factories, life was almost as hard. As G M Trevelyan says, these were 'barracks for cheap labour, not homes for citizens'. They would typically work a fourteen- to sixteen-hour day, six days a week, and many were not even adequately clothed or fed. Descendants of the outlaws around Hathersage now coughed their lives away over needle-grinding machines that were powered by the waters of Hood Brook. Their life expectancy was only ten years, with nearly a fifth of those who started in their teens dying in their twenties from a form of silicosis caused by inhaling metal particles and gritstone dust, their noses quite literally to the grindstone.

The machine-breaking 'Luddites' of Nottingham (led by a Ned Ludd, calling himself 'The King', from headquarters in Sherwood Forest) could do nothing to stop the juggernaut of industry. Everywhere people were drawn to the factories to become anonymous cogs in the new economic machine. 'Men are grown mechanical in head and heart, as well as hand,' wrote Thomas Carlyle in 1829. 'Their whole efforts, attachments, opinions, turn on mechanism and are of a mechanical character.'

Where the Church might have helped, it hindered. The Puritan work ethic of the Age of the Enlightenment was now underpinned by the 'Methodism' of John Wesley. 'Wherever God erects a house of prayer', the outspoken Defoe had said two generations before, 'the Devil always builds a chapel there'; and now, unbelievably, as if from another age, Wesley was speaking of witches and possession by the devil and insisting that the only route to salvation was through thrift, abstinence and hard work. Far from trying to stem the tide of child labour, he declared that, for the sake of everlasting life, children *should* work.

Not that the tough old people of the Peak were to be so easily manipulated. When Wesley visited Matlock Bath in 1761, he had a hostile reception. 'Why do you talk thus of Faith?' they demanded. 'Stuff, nonsense!' Generally, the old miners – as 'daring and desperate' as ever – distrusted the clergy, calling them 'black dragoons'. And with good reason. Many of the clergy were active magistrates and, before the days of a police force, rural England was in the absolute sway of the Justices of the Peace. It was a nightmare scenario, what today we would call a Catch-22. All the Justices were squires and Tory partisans, and all public meetings, which were not licensed by them, were banned. The working man was hemmed in on every side, with no rights at all. As Bishop Horsley put it baldly in 1795: 'The mass of the people have nothing to do with the laws but to obey them.'

The year 1816 was an exceptionally bad year in the Peak – 'the worst year which was ever recollected' – with exceptionally cold and wet weather, higher rents, a 40 per cent increase in the cost of bread, and a fourfold increase in crime. Various 'illegal' political societies were formed, and a peaceful March of the Blanketeers was halted by troops in Ashbourne. The ever more repressive Tory government of Lord Liverpool suspended habeas corpus, and, shortly afterwards, the South Wingfield area of the Peak was shaken by a 'great earthquake'. But as in difficult times in the past, it is doubtful if anyone heeded the warnings.

Signs of imminent trouble occurred again at South Wingfield the next year, with the burning of the local squire-cum-magistrate's hayricks. Behind the scenes a secret committee of militant reformers – a needle-maker, a framework knitter, a bankrupt farmer and an out-of-work stockinger called Jeremiah Brandreth – had been meeting in a barn near Pentrich plotting a 'revolution'. The plan was simple: having taken

Nottingham, where 16,000 men were said to be ready to back them, they would march on to London and set up a new, 'provision' government ... Commitment must be total, and any 'vermin' who opposed eradicated. Brandreth expressed it in verse:

> Every man his skill must try,
> He must turn out and not deny;
> No bloody soldier must he dread,
> He must turn out and fight for bread.

In the early hours of 10 June, the revolutionaries, armed with guns and pitchforks and numbering less than a hundred, set out from South Wingfield and marched on the Butterley Ironworks, terrorising the neighbourhood and murdering one man in the process. On their arrival at the foundry gates they were confronted by George Goodwin, the manager, who demanded to know what they were about.

'We want your men,' said Brandreth.

'You shall not have them,' said Goodwin. 'Disperse. The law will be too strong for you. You are going with halters about your necks, and you will all be hanged. Go home.'

He was more or less right. Once they had been rounded up, twenty of the culprits were transported, and on 7 November, Brandreth and two others were hanged and beheaded on Nun's Green in front of Derby gaol. The executioner held up their severed heads before a large crowd, which included the poet Shelley, who was sufficiently provoked to write an anonymous pamphlet about 'the corpse of British Liberty'. But the truth is that this harebrained insurrection had gained little local support. Such an ill-calculated piece of collective action was altogether repellent to the self-reliant Peakrill.

Much more to their way of thinking was the style of the good-humoured Ebenezer Elliott, the famed 'Corn Law Rhymer' of Sheffield, who 'loved a country walk as sincerely as he hated the Corn Laws and the Tories'. He was as likely to turn to drink, or climbing hills, as he was to political action. Indeed, he recommended 'old ale' as 'the best and only stimulant on which to climb', and this undoubtedly affected the quality of his verse:

> Now having drunk of jolly ale enough
> To climb Win Hill is worth ambition—yea,
> Ambition, e'en made of jolly stuff,
> Should drink strong ale, or never will he say
> To rival climbers, 'Follow on my way!'...

JEREMIAH BRANDRETH - A TRAITOR.

Published March 1 1821 by G. Smeeton, St Martins Church Yard.

Reproduced with permission from Derby Local Studies Library

The bleak portals of Winnats
Pass in February

STEAM AND SPEED

With the enormous growth of industry in the great industrial centres of Sheffield and
Manchester on its flanks, the Peak remained a serious barrier to communication. Always
in between. In 1800 the fastest way from Sheffield to Manchester, a 48-mile turnpike
route via the Winnats Pass, still took 16 hours. 'By heavens!' said Samuel Taylor Coleridge,
facing the prospect, 'a tortoise would outgallop us!'

But the Peak people were used to such difficulties. Sometimes over thirty passengers
would be crammed on to a coach which was legally restricted to twelve. 'Comfort is out

Winnats Pass.

In 1758, the first year in which the Winnats Pass turnpike had been opened, an eloping couple on the way to Peak Forest (where the vicar could conduct marriages without banns) were robbed and murdered in the Pass and their bodies thrown into the nearby Speedwell Mine

of the question,' a traveller reported in 1817. 'Annoyances include the smell of putrid game and fish, the long and chilly waits for connecting coaches, and the immense loads of luggage carried on the roof to the danger of passengers.' Winter journeys were particularly hazardous. Outside passengers, who had been known to freeze to death, were advised to 'drink a tankard of good ale cold from the tap, and rub their hands, ears and faces with snow immediately before they start'.

Large sections of the Derwent Valley were still, in the early nineteenth century, more or less impassable except on foot or horseback, and the few awkward, narrow bridges across the river were frequently swept away. There was no road of any kind along the valley bottom between Belper and Cromford until 1817. Soon after this, however, the process of 'macadaming' began, using small stones and, later, tar to solidify the road surface. For the first time, stagecoaches could literally hurtle along at full gallop – but in the very hour of their glory, when they had finally come of age as a mode of transport, they were eclipsed by the steam engine.

In 1825, the year in which the first railway in Britain was opened in County Durham (on which Stephenson's 'Rocket' would soon reach the startling velocity of 27 miles per hour), Josias Jessop started work on a futuristic 'waggonway' following a seemingly impossible route over 33 miles of the White Peak to Whaley Bridge. Reaching a height of 1,300 feet, it passed daringly close to such ancient burial sites as Harboro, Minninglow and Gib Hill. The first section, the Sheep Pasture Incline from the Cromford Canal, climbed 987 feet at an extraordinary gradient of 1 in 8. Up this and other steep inclines the waggons were hauled on chains by stationary steam winding engines. 'Who would have thought of a railway over such acclivities and apparently inaccessible tracts?' William Adam exclaimed in amazement, and another compared the feat with the mad Archimedes' attempt to 'square the circle'. But, as was clear from his company motto – Divina Palladis Arte ('By the Divine Skill of Pallas') – Jessop had the Greek god of engineering on his side, and by 1841 his Cromford and High Peak Railway was carrying steam locomotives across the Peak. But they still had to be hauled up the steepest inclines, which remained a very slow and cumbersome process.

In 1836 Mr 'Rocket' himself, the famed George Stephenson, arrived in the valley to construct a railway northwards from Derby to Leeds via Ambergate and Chesterfield. Working night and day, seven days a week, with a team of 1,500 navvies, he blasted his way up the side of the Derwent. As an engineering feat it was compared by a contemporary with Napoleon's military road across the Simplon Pass, and Ruskin looked aghast at embankments that were 'vaster than the walls of Babylon'.

But there was still no direct railway link across the Peak from Derby to Manchester. By 1849 the line up the Derwent Valley had been extended northwards as far as Rowsley, but an enormous obstacle – greater even than the engineering difficulties – remained:

The last of the major turnpikes in the Peak was the Snake Pass, built by Thomas Telford and completed in 1821, which took a more direct route between Sheffield and Manchester than Winnats Pass, following a line close to the old Roman road from Navio to Ardotalia. Reaching a height of 1680 feet, this was one of the highest turnpikes in Britain. The name 'Snake' has nothing to do with the road's sinuous route but comes from the snake in the Duke of Devonshire's crest

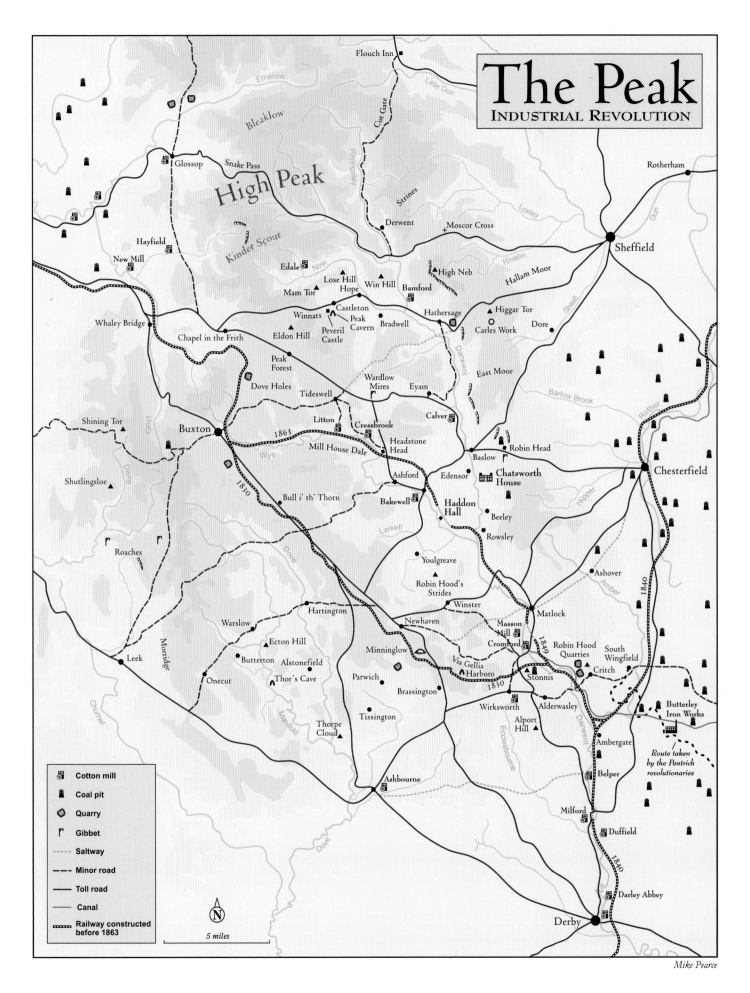

The Peak
INDUSTRIAL REVOLUTION

Flouch Inn

Etherow

Bleaklow

Cut Gate

Little Don

Wrongsley

Glossop

Snake Pass

High Peak

Strines

Derwent

Moscor Cross

Loxley

Rotherham

Don

Sheffield

Hayfield

Kinder Scout

New Mill

Now

Edale

Rivelin

High Neb

Hallam Moor

Whaley Bridge

Chapel in the Frith

Lose Hill
Hope

Mam Tor

Win Hill

Bamford

Higgar Tor

Hathersage

Sheaf

Dore

Winnats
Castleton
Peak
Cavern

Bradwell

Carles Work

Eldon Hill

Peveril
Castle

Peak
Forest

East Moor

Shining Tor

Dove Holes

Wardlow
Mires

Eyam

Barlow Brook

Rother

Tideswell

Litton

Cressbrook

Calver

Govt

Buxton

1863

Headstone
Head

Robin Head

Wye

Mill House Dale

Baslow

Chesterfield

Shutlingsloe

1830

Ashford

Edensor

Chatsworth
House

Dane

Bull i' th' Thorn

Bakewell

Haddon
Hall

Beeley

Hipper

Rowsley

Roaches

Larkell

Dove

Youlgreave

Ashover

Robin Hood's
Strides

Amber

Warslow

Hartington

Winster

Matlock

Morridge

Newhaven

Masson
Mill

Robin Hood
Quarries

South
Wingfield

Leek

Ecton Hill

Cromford

Butterton

Alstonefield

Minninglow

Via Gellia

Stonnis

Critch

Onecut

Thor's Cave

Parwich

Harboro

1849

1840

Churnet

Brassington

1830

Wirksworth

Alderwasley

Butterley
Iron Works

Tissington

Eccesbourne

Alport
Hill

Darwent

Route taken
by the Pentrich
revolutionaries

Thorpe
Cloud

Manifold

Ambergate

Dove

Ashbourne

Belper

Milford

1840

Duffield

Darley Abbey

Derby

Legend
- Cotton mill
- Coal pit
- Quarry
- Gibbet
- Saltway
- Minor road
- Toll road
- Canal
- Railway constructed before 1863

N

5 miles

Mike Pearce

the Dukes of Rutland and Devonshire, through whose land the only two possible routes lay, absolutely refused to contemplate it. Eventually, after three years of protracted wrangling, a deal was struck in 1863 with the Duke of Rutland for a route through the Wye Valley. But with stringent conditions: the railway must be buried in a tunnel in the hillside behind Haddon Hall, not a single tree must be touched, and the company must provide the duke with his own station at Bakewell. In the imagery of the rival dukes' family crests, the traditionally sly Devonshire snake had been completely outpaced by the Rutland peacock; and now the Duke of Devonshire, who thus far had wanted no part of it, demanded a station all of his own – which was duly constructed at Hassop, scarcely a mile from Bakewell.

With the way now clear for the most spectacular railway in England, a new kind of fire-breathing demon burst through Headstone Head into Demon's Dale near Hob's House, and made its outlandish way through the crag-bound gorge of the Wye Valley to Buxton. Ruskin wrote in shock and horror:

> There was a rocky valley between Buxton and Bakewell, once upon a time, divine as the vale of Tempe; you might have seen the gods there morning and evening – Apollo and all the sweet Muses of the Light, walking in fair procession on the lawns of it, and to and fro among the pinnacles of its crags. You cared neither for gods nor grass, but for cash. You enterprised a railroad through the valley, you blasted its rocks away, heaped thousands of tons of shale into its lovely stream. The valley is gone, and the gods with it; and now, every fool in Buxton can be at Bakewell in half-an-hour, and every fool in Bakewell at Buxton.

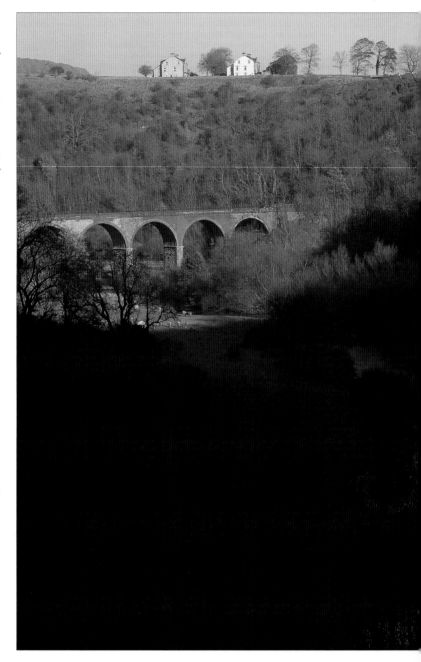

Ruskin's 'vale of Tempe': Monsal Dale and the railway viaduct below Headstone Head (now Monsal Head), as seen from Hob's House

DAY OF WRATH

... Nothing can resist us. We war with rude Nature; and, by our resistless engines, come off always victorious, and loaded with spoils ... We are Giants in physical power: in a deeper than metaphorical sense, we are Titans ...

Thomas Carlyle, *Signs of the Times,* 1829

The great lumbering machine of industry, which had already made such scars and inroads into the Peak landscape, was now devouring the very rock itself, biting the hand that fed it. All the railway and bridge construction required the opening up of enormous new gritstone quarries, in addition to those already providing millstones for flour mills, and grindstones for lead-crushing and cutlery. This novel variety of 'stones with holes' became a totem in the Peak for the new materialistic religion of industrial

capitalism. Soon all the stones with holes that any pagan captain of industry could wish for in his profanest dreams were at his disposal.

Where once there had been Celtic fire festivals, now there were coke ovens belching smoke and flame into the night sky, creating a scene more 'truly sublime and awful' than any that any artist had ever seen before or imagined, 'even in the regions of everlasting punishment'. The air, in this new 'kingdom of Vulcan', was full of sulphur and gunpowder, and a perpetual pall of smoke hung over the limekilns of Stoney Middleton and Ambergate, which flamed at night like a line of miniature volcanoes, blackening the crags and killing the very lichen itself.

The giant wheels of progress, which had mutated from the patter of waterwheels to the harsh grating of grindstones, had now become the circles of hell, with the worker bound like Lear on a wheel of fire, as he was dragged ever deeper into the hell-hole of heavy industry – or shackled, like the apprentices at Litton who could not keep pace with their machines, to the beams above them. Incarcerated in a new world of stridulant noise: the cacophonous roar of blasting engines, the thumping of welding hammers, and the grinding and banging of heavy machinery. The whole landscape reverberating with the thunder of explosions and the rumble of stone wheels, as pairs of millstones were rolled down the Derwent's wooded slopes on their overstressed axles.

No chance of hearing the 'birdes song' now!

And here it comes – the Jabberwock, with eyes of flame, whiffling through the tulgey wood! – Brunton's steam-powered 'Walking Locomotive', hissing and puffing slowly up the Butterley Gang Road from the Cromford Canal, propelled stiffly forward on its jointed legs like a shuffling invalid. And on the opposite side of the valley, sudden cries of alarm as a cable snaps and *a whole train* – a brake van and a waggonload of limestone – comes hurtling backwards down the Sheep Pasture Incline, the whine of its wheels rising to an almighty crescendo – and then, in an awful moment of silence, it is flying, disjointed and wild, clean through the air, all nineteen tons of it, right across the canal, to crash with a mighty roar of disgorging blocks into the soft pasture beyond.

And in the stunned hush that follows – above the wheezing and sighing of the distant Newcomen engines, and the hoarse croaking and coughing of the nailers and the cries of the children – and the mad King George playing the harpsichord and muttering 'What, what, what?' – a clamour of urgent, angry voices, contending. The one-time champion of progress and minimal government, the Derby philosopher Herbert Spencer – the very man who had invented the phrase 'the survival of the fittest' – now crying out that 'No one can be perfectly free till *all* are free', and that individualism can only come after an era of socialism and war. Then the quieter, quivering voice of Ruskin, saying, 'The foundations of society were never yet shaken as they are at this day ... there is a pestilential air at the bottom of it', and suddenly exploding with anger – 'You think this a lucrative process of exchange, *you fools* everywhere!' And finally the stentorian tones of Carlyle ringing out into the future:

> The time is sick and out of joint. Many things have reached their height; and it is a wise adage that tells us, *the darkest hour is nearest the dawn.*

With their proximity to the Cromford Canal, the enormous Robin Hood and Duke's Quarries at Whatstandwell provided for nearly 100 years (from 1830) the most accessible high quality building stone in the Peak. Who would ever guess now that this was the provenance of Birmingham and Leicester Jails, and of the Victoria Docks in London?

Progress is not an accident but a necessity ... It is a part of nature.

Herbert Spencer, Derby-born philosopher, 1850

8 The Great Escape

1886: PUTTRELL'S PROGRESS

The wheels of progress continue to turn, and we find ourselves once again in a new world that has changed beyond all recognition. Epoch-making Reform Bills have given the working man the vote, Factory Acts have vastly improved his working conditions and abolished child labour, Trade Unions Acts have enabled collective bargaining, Education Bills have introduced primary state education and County Council Acts have instituted rural self-government. It has also been a period of enormous scientific progress with such great advances as the invention of the telephone, the internal combustion engine and vaccines, to name but three. With Britain now the richest country in the world, it is little wonder that the concept of industrial progress has acquired the status of a religious faith.

Yet there is some disquiet. The socialist poet and philosopher Edward Carpenter, who has recently moved to Millthorp in the heart of old outlaw country to the east of Grindleford, is even now working on a book called *Civilization: Its Cause and Cure* in which he will compare the process of civilization to 'a kind of disease'. But, while he is hankering after some long-lost world of rural crafts that has probably never existed, city folk are embracing the benefits of industry with enthusiasm; for it is industry, after all, which has given them a new mobility and the means to escape to their ancestral hills.

Two major new railways between Sheffield and Manchester, created primarily for industrial purposes, with stations at Crowden, Grindleford, Hathersage and Edale, have suddenly brought the heart of the Peak within easy reach of the grim, smoke-filled conurbations of Manchester, Sheffield and Derby.

This steep and awkward landscape, which first attracted the industrialists for its water power and building materials, has now revealed a whole new kind of wealth in the rock; for the very hard variety of sandstone, which has already proved so suitable for making grindstones, has now been found to provide unforeseen sporting opportunities, such that the enthusiast might argue that this was its true destiny all along …

It is as if, with the new freedom, and the recent remarkable improvement in the weather (for the last few summers have been the warmest on record), there has come a subtle shift in attitude, the perception that adventure is perhaps as important as industry.

And so, on a fine summer's morning in 1886, we can easily imagine a certain James William Puttrell, a small, energetic young man from a Sheffield silversmith factory, striding up the hill from Deepcar Station with one of his work colleagues, whom he has finally persuaded to join him in a mad new sporting activity. They are wearing hobnailed boots and carrying a rope …

◄ Edensor village in the late autumn. This idyllic Victorian rural scene is largely man-made: the present-day village of Edensor was built in 'Capability' Brown's Chatsworth Park in 1838-42 by Joseph Paxton for the immensely cultured, 'funny and sad' bachelor, the 'unDevonshirelike' Sixth Duke of Devonshire

'Puttrell's Progress',
Wharncliffe, which is believed
to date from as early as 1886,
is still graded Severe. The crag's
ancient name, 'Querncliffe', is
said to derive from the early
production here of 'querns', or
primitive grindstones

Climber: Steve Dean

*… The great climb in this group is the hand-traverse across the
rock-face above the cavern's mouth. I am told that it is bad
form to name climbs after individuals; but I am unwilling to
relinquish the title of 'Puttrell's Progress' that has been
bestowed on this particular piece of work. Mr J W Puttrell is a
capable and daring cragsman … This hand-traverse is at
present his monopoly, and is one of the most sensational climbs
to be found at the Crags.*

C F Cameron, 1902

The 'Crazy Pinnacle' in Tegness Quarry above Grindleford, first climbed by Puttrell in the late 1890s with Ernest Baker. They were among the founder members of the Climbers' Club in 1898, and the Peak-centred Kyndwr Club in 1900

Climber: Tom Gifford

… above Grindleford we found a gritstone pinnacle, about 40 feet high, which had been left by the quarrymen. It had smooth vertical sides and a crown of shattered blocks that actually overhung; but finding one angle thin enough to be gripped by arms and legs, we resolved to try this … The doubtful rib held, we swarmed up and over it, shuddering for a moment when we felt it quiver, and in three minutes were on the top.

Ernest Baker, 1898

1909 FURTHER AFIELD

Over the next decade, using the railway, and often walking vast distances, Puttrell and his friends systematically explored the eastern edges, as well as making daring ascents of the crumbling face of Mam Tor and of the first Very Severe on limestone in 1898. By the turn of the century they were turning their attention to remoter crags such as Kinder Downfall, the Roaches and Hen Cloud. First to try to climb the sheer bastion of Hen Cloud was John Laycock of the Climbers' Club, who arrived late one afternoon in 1909 with his friend A R Thomson …

As shapely and dignified a summit as any 3,000 ft sgurr in the Western Highlands; its long ridge bristles with sharp teeth, and the noble cliff fronting it is as imposing in contour, as seen against the clouds, as if its extreme height of 150 ft or so were magnified fourfold.

Ernest Baker, 1903

'The Arête', Hen Cloud, first climbed in about 1902

Climber: Chris Thorp

◀ Hen Cloud on a late evening in May. The climber is on the route 'K2', first climbed in 1927, some 25 feet to the right of Laycock's 'Central Climb'. Laycock would perhaps be gratified to know that his climb today warrants the grade of Very Severe

Thomson found much difficulty and prepared not to follow. The light began to fade, but I made my way up the next two pitches, and finally stuck at the top wall, where I unsuccessfully tried a line somewhat on the left of the present route. I spent some time here, and twilight fell. Alone on a new climb, and in the gathering gloom, I found difficulty in descending the lower pitches. Accordingly I remained on the ledge and Thomson went off for assistance. Night fell, a cold night of stars, but I was quite happy. After what seemed (and must have been) hours, a wavering light and tinkle of metal, mixed with noises of stumbling and language, apprised me of the approach of relief. Thereafter Thomson and the sturdy chauffeur hauled me to the top. Not everyone has been benighted on Gritstone, and though one ought to be ashamed of want of prudence, the episode is delightful to me in retrospect.

Gritstone has its romance no less than granite.

John Laycock, on the first ascent of 'Central Route', in 1909

◀ Climbing the 'Matterhorn Ridge' in the Winnats Pass. The original caption of this undated photograph reads: 'The climb was made more difficult today as snow & rain fell during the climb and fingers were num with cold before the top was reached.'

Grant Jarvis collection

... the careful limestoner will not here pull on the projections, but will, for about 120 feet, raise himself by pressing downwards on them ... The situations on this climb are remarkably airy; and neither it nor the Elbow ridge is suitable for a windy day.

Henry Bishop, 1910

Although most of the climbing development was on the Millstone Grit, such that the Peak was said by 1914 to be the leading 'laboratory of technique' in Britain, tentative forays were also made onto the utterly different, and much more dangerous, Mountain Limestone of the Winnats Pass (above), as well as on to the altogether friendlier Dolomitic Limestone to be found around the village of Brassington (right).

Apart from the modest Henry Bishop, who 'rarely published any results of his labours', the leading team at this time was the formidable triumvirate of John Laycock and his close friends Siegfried Herford and Stanley Jeffcoat. With Herford very much the technical star and leader, they produced several climbs, here and in the Lake District, which were many years ahead of their time in terms of difficulty.

The strongest personality of the three was the 'amiable giant' from Buxton, Stanley Jeffcoat. 'Tall and strong, enthusiastic, able to climb anything, of a sunny disposition, and always bubbling over with spirits', his popularity was such that it was said that a letter addressed to 'Jeff, Buxton' would get to him.

▶ Jeffcoat's Pinnacle, near Brassington, climbed in 1912, just one of four notable rock features named after the 'amiable giant' from Buxton

Climber: John Lumb

Laughter was generally to be heard when he was in the neighbourhood.

A R Thomson

I was at a country tennis tournament the day we declared war on Germany. Young men and maidens, grey-moustached veterans, pale-faced curates, dear old ladies: one and all expressed relief and thankfulness. 'I was so afraid Grey would climb down at the last moment ... I didn't think the old man had the grit.' Such was the talk over the teacups. It was the same whichever way you looked. Railway porters, cabmen, workmen riding home upon their bicycles, farm labourers eating their bread and cheese beside the hedge: they had the faces of men to whom good tidings had come. Of course, not a soul dreamt the war was going to last more than a few months ...

Jerome K Jerome reflecting in 1926

WAR AND DEPRESSION

The 'war to end all wars', which was going to be 'over by Christmas', but lasted five years, cost a million British lives. A whole generation was literally decimated on the battlefields of France; and it was inevitable that among the casualties would be some of the very best rock-climbers, including both Herford and Jeffcoat. These great names, already attached for ever to the Peakland rock, were now prematurely etched into the stone of War Memorials in Wasdale and Great Longstone. Laycock never got over the loss of his closest friends and emigrated soon afterwards to Singapore.

The most talented climbers to step into this enormous vacuum were Fred Pigott and Morley Wood, who had both distinguished themselves in the war; and, like the Herford, Jeffcoat and Laycock team, they too were soon to make climbing history in the mountains of Britain, as well as in their home training ground of the Peak.

The wiry 25-year-old Fred Pigott was the natural leader around whom everything revolved, while the quieter Morley Wood, eight years his senior, who had been climbing since 1909, was technically at least his equal and the perfect anchor man. They both made a lasting impression on all those who knew them. Pigott is remembered vividly by Arthur Birtwistle today as 'a great chap: amusing, and absolutely unflappable'; while Morley Wood is described by Frank Kiernan as 'a charming man. Very courteous, very calm and very polite. A very pleasant character whom everybody liked'.

▶ 'Sand Buttress' at Black Rocks, Cromford, climbed by Fred Pigott and Morley Wood in 1920. Before the advent of modern protection devices this superb VS was a very bold climb of its standard

Climber: John Cutcliffe

Climber: Adam Long

Legs are a positive encumbrance as there are no footholds on the traverse from the left, and it is exceedingly difficult to get the lower half of the body on to the ledge at the end of this hand-traverse.

Morley Wood describing 'Kelly's Overhang'

Harry Kelly, after whom this fierce challenge on High Neb is now named, was an early enthusiast for 'the adhesive delights of plimsolls'. But here they failed him, and it was left to 'the presiding spirit of those days', Rice Kemper Evans, the ebullient American Vice-Consul in Sheffield, to make the first successful ascent on a top rope around 1920. He had a special way with words; indeed it was his fondness for 'cute little laybacks' that gave the climbing world a term that became universal.

It was inevitable that Fred Pigott and Morley Wood would soon become the central core of a small circle of the Stanage enthusiasts. Morley, with his reputation for being a 'good second', has almost certainly been underrated by climbing historians. Pigott himself described him as being 'in the true sense adventurous', as well as combining great strength with 'a considerable measure of delicacy'. But he was not dangerous, for in the whole time they climbed together Pigott never once saw him slip.

Morley first climbed Kelly's Overhang on a top rope in 1924 and then returned in 1926 with Pigott to make the first lead, at the age of 39, of what was to be technically the hardest rock climb in the Peak for many years (now accurately graded HVS 5b). It was also notable for being one of the first occasions on which a double rope was used, as is recorded in a well-known photograph of Morley Wood at this precise point on the first ascent. But, despite this photograph, and one of Pigott seconding a few minutes later, Morley Wood's lead has always been held in some doubt because of its remarkable difficulty. Perhaps the fact that the pioneers referred to the climb as 'the Inaccessible Buttress' rather than 'Kelly's Overhang' goes some way towards explaining why it did not appear in any guidebook for many years.

Eric Byne was later to describe this as a 'Golden Period' at Stanage. 'Easy access, friendly gamekeepers, and delightful days picnicking amongst the millstones at the foot of High Neb and wandering rubber-shod up new unscratched routes on splendidly sound steep rock.'

One is badly out of balance while advancing the left hand. However, the balance is rectified as soon as the left is landed, and the right hand thrown over the nose of the overhang encounters one of these exceptionally gratifying grips invariably conducive to devotional expression.

A perfectly good foot position offers for the right; it is a delusion; in fact its sole sphere of usefulness in this world is for the left foot.

Two small holes, about on the waist line, give the steadying grip necessary to throw the right foot well out and up to a toe-hold on a level with the hips. Rise on that toe – Pigott and Pavlova do it beautifully ...

Rice K Evans, an early connoisseur of the crux move, 1923

This boulder, not mentioned in any climbing guidebook, is situated above the road down Bar Brook at the northern end of Gardom's Edge. Little over a mile away, a very similar, but larger, feature called 'Gun Rock' overlooking the road beside the Robin Hood Inn was used as the gibbet which gave Gibbet Moor its name. This particular prow was probably too small ever to have been used for anything less healthy than climbing

Grant Jarvis collection

Frank Elliott recalls how he started to climb in 1929:

'I'd got a very, very old book on mountaineering and rock climbing – very, very ancient, it must have been Victorian – and it advised in that using a cotton rope. It recommended forty feet for two people.

'I didn't know anything about belays, or anything at all. At first we didn't use a sling or anything. We just belayed from the shoulder. Pretty unsafe, but that's what we did. You'd hold them. They'd say, "I'm falling," and then they'd climb up the rope. We never fell off leading.

'As an apprentice I got only about five shillings a week, so the only clothing we could afford was second-hand army clothing. Which was usually khaki trousers and a khaki jacket and a khaki shirt. More or less what they were wearing in the '14 war. But then as I got more money, when I'd once served my apprenticeship, I went to a place in Sheffield who made clothes for working men – mole-skins and cords. And they had a plus-two cord suit with a Norfolk jacket. It were a quite rare one.

'Tower Face' at Wharncliffe, first climbed by Eric Byne and Frank Burgess in 1933

Climber: Mick Wrigley

'Puttrell was the leading light at Wharncliffe. I contacted him myself when I was about 19. He seemed quite pleased. He was quite old and sort of shuffling around. I think he had a beard. He was pretty isolated by then. Most of the people he'd climbed with had died. He was frightfully keen on it still and very friendly. He lent me this typewritten guide, so I climbed everything. I just went through it systematically.

'The rock was terribly dirty. When we went there we'd come back absolutely filthy. Our trousers were in shreds, and everything was just black. It was from all the factories and the smelting in that area. There were huge blast furnaces below. At night all these flares used to be coming up at Deepcar.'

We may note in passing that, long before the industrial revolution, a legendary fire-breathing 'Dragon of Wantley' had once ravaged the countryside around Wharncliffe.

◂ The remarkable 'Cave Gully Wall' at Stanage, first climbed on a snowy Sunday in 1932 by Alf Bridge. A very powerful climber, Bridge was famous for turning enormous falls into spectacular jumps. 'I've seen him leap off and run down like a sheep,' says Dick Brown

Climber: Steve Dean

'Stanage Edge was fairly near to my home. I lived in Ecclesall, near Sheffield. So I could walk out. We never saw anybody else out there. We didn't know anything about routes, we didn't know they had names. We just went along and said, "Oh, that looks possible," and had a go at it. But around about 1930, I should think, or '29, I met this chap, Kelly. He was quite old by then – a small chap. He wasn't climbing much at all. I saw him fairly regularly. He used to come wandering up on his own. He showed us the various routes, and gave us the names, and we led them – I led most of them. And he came up on our rope.'

Frank Elliott, who was to make several very hard first ascents here in the next few years, including a slab that was later graded E2, remembering Stanage in 1930

'Eventually, about 1929, I got in touch with the Nottingham Mountaineering Club, and there were one or two people there who were fairly influential, and they'd got permission to climb on Gardom's Rocks. Nobody ever climbed there at all. Absolutely strictly private. You couldn't get on there at all. But this chap, Joe Allen in the Nottingham Club, he knew the owner – his father had connections with nearly all the lace factories in Nottingham – and he gave just us permission to climb there. Nobody else. He used to turn everybody else off. So we really pioneered the rocks.

'Occasionally we went to other crags without permission. We were quite often chased off. It could be very unpleasant. I remember getting beaten up fairly badly at one time. We weren't climbing, we were coming up over Featherbed Moss – there's an old road there that was a short cut. It was open country, and they saw us, and came across to us, and just let into us with sticks. They didn't say anything. That happened in the north in those days. There was quite a lot of that – on Kinder Scout and Bleaklow and so on.

'High Neb was very difficult. You weren't allowed to go along there, but we used to try, and when we heard or saw the gamekeepers, we'd scoot off again. They were a little bit abusive, but they never really hit you or anything, but they used to insist on you getting off quick. So High Neb became impossible. I think Froggatt was impossible as well. We did walk along the top, but never did any climbing there to talk about at all.'

Frank Elliott reminiscing in 1996

Peter Harding, who was himself one of the leading pioneers of the next generation, climbing 'Elliott's Buttress' at Gardom's Edge in October 1995

► Frank Elliott, great-great-great grandson of Ebenezer Elliott, the 'Corn Law Rhymer', and his wife Nan at their home in Kent in 1996. Frank was most anxious to stress to me that climbing in the Peak was only one aspect of a very full life, which has included among other things Antarctic exploration (Polar Medal) and a traverse of the North Face of the Eiger in 1946

'I left Sheffield in 1931. I went on leave and got myself a job at Rolls Royce, and eventually landed up at the Dagenham Ford Motor Company. I was sorry in some ways – I thought that's the end of my rock-climbing. But I had a car, and I was able, in my position at Ford, to finish work on a Friday at about 2 o'clock and not go back till Monday at 2 o'clock. So I got long week-ends. I used to plan to get up to the Peak once a month, I think. About three or four of us would go, and we'd take it in turns with the driving. It wasn't so difficult in those days.'

◄ The imposing 'Great Ridge' (now called 'Aurora') at Stoney Middleton, was climbed years ahead of its time in 1933 by Elliott, Dover and Ellis. Today it is a polished VS classic, at the upper limit of its grade

'It took us all day to do it. We kept going up a bit, and down a bit … There was a lot of gardening. It was pretty rotten. There was tons of loose rock. We were chucking it down all the time … It starts with quite a sheer buttress, and we had an awful job to get up that. I wasn't in the lead all the time, I think Gilbert Ellis did a bit of leading as well. He was very short, but tremendously strong. And Dover was on that climb, both of them. Yes, the three of us.

'We had one of these Belfast ropes by then. It's a hemp. We used to get them from Ireland. Half-inch. We never used pitons – for years and years. When I think back, we took a lot of chances.'

'One unlucky day, grouse-shooting became a pastime for the idle rich, and the policy of shutting up the open wild gradually began …

The day was just ending as I was descending
Through Grindsbrook just by Upper Tor,
When a voice cried, 'Hey, you!', in the way keepers do,
(He'd the worst face that ever I saw).

… He called me a louse and said 'Think of the grouse',
Well, I thought but I still couldn't see
Why old Kinder Scout and the moors round about
Couldn't take both the poor grouse and me.

From *The Manchester Rambler* by Ewan MacColl, press officer on the
Kinder Trespass of 1932

Kinder Scout from Hollin
Head on the lower slopes of
Sandy Heys, scene of the
famous Mass Trespass in April
1932 which resulted in the
imprisonment of five of the
ringleaders. There were further
Mass Trespasses in Abbey
Brook and at Stanage Edge in
the autumn, and protest rallies
in Winnats Pass and at Jacob's
Ladder

… Complete freedom of access may be delayed, but it will come inevitably; the day when every barrier must be removed, to meet the lawful necessities of the people.'

Ernest Baker, 1926

Kinder Downfall in February

No sacred mountain in Tibet is more strictly guarded. It must not be walked upon without permission given in writing; it must not be photographed without permission of the owner; even to print his name may be an infringement of his rights.

Edwin Royce of the Manchester Ramblers' Federation, 1938

Many years of frustration were to pass before Baker's dream of 'complete freedom of access' was realised in 1949. From our privileged position at the end of the twentieth century we may marvel at the meanness embodied in a final pitiful and inglorious remnant of the 'chase' in which birds that can scarcely fly are gunned down with multiple bullets. The peak of this bloodlust occurred in August 1913 when 1,421 brace were shot by nine guns in the course of a single day on the Broomhead Moors.

◀ 'Upper Tor Wall' above Grindsbrook, Kinder Scout, first climbed by Arthur Birtwistle in 1937

Climber: Mike Pearce

▶ Arthur Birtwistle in Grindsbrook in November 1997, with the crag of Upper Tor on the skyline behind

'I had a friend, Philip Brookbank in the Rucksack Club, who knew Kinder like the back of his hand. It started with him saying I'll take you out and show you some crags – because there were no guide books. This would have been 1937. He took me to Upper Tor and I saw Upper Tor Wall. What actually happened was Philip wouldn't climb it – he said, 'No, that's much too hard for me!' So I did the first part solo, up to the break near the top, and Philip traversed on and gave me a belay. I didn't like the looks of that flake at the top, I thought it might come away.

'With those things, soloing or leading didn't make any odds. I don't think I ever used running belays on gritstone, ever. Part of the technique of climbing at that time was you had to be able to climb down what you'd climbed up, and I don't think that I've ever done anything that I couldn't have climbed down at a pinch.'

That's all gone out of the window with modern protection! Have you seen the gear that climbers use nowadays?

'You know, I was a gymnast and I was using chalk in the gym, on the horizontal bar. Magnesium carbonate, the same stuff they use on the rock now – and we never, ever thought of using it on the rock! It was the same with nuts and wedges. I mean, climbing was just you, as you are, and the rocks and the weather. And that was it.'

When you're walking on Kinder do you ever talk to people coming up these routes you did?

'No ... no ...'

So they've no idea that the pioneer is watching them?

'No, I just keep my mouth shut and watch!'

Arthur Birtwistle in conversation, 1997

'Ravenstones was a favourite crag of mine. All the cracks had been done but none of the ridges; and the two big ridges were the Pulpit Ridge and the one on the right of it. I did Pulpit Ridge first. I found the top part of it hard, getting to a horizontal crack. It's quite thin. But it's simple, it's a friction job. I was wearing a pair of pumps with very thin, hard rubber soles. You got them very, very tight – a size too small. The best type was a shilling from Woolworth's. I think they were sixpence originally. They didn't last long, they fell apart. And they were hopeless if it was wet. I climbed an awful lot in socks.'

Were there other people climbing at your standard that you were aware of?

'Well, obviously there were quite a lot of people climbing at the same standard, but you were more in a cocoon. You know, communication wasnt like it was later; I mean, we didn't go much in pubs before the war. It was a different world – we didn't have enough money you know, that was the problem. Beer wasn't very expensive, but … it was almost a different world really.'

What do you feel about the way climbing is going nowadays?

'Well, it seems to me that you can almost sum up the difference, even though we were climbing on gritstone, ticking things off, we always felt that we were mountaineers. We didn't feel we were just rock climbers. We climbed in the Alps and did a lot of gullies under ice, and a load of that sort of climbing. I mean, that was all part of the game. You weren't just rock climbers. That's the big difference, I think. You know, that's one reason why nobody climbed on limestone – most of the limestone crags are not on the mountain; and, as I say, we all regarded ourselves as mountaineers.'

So you never tried the limestone at all?

'No, I never climbed on limestone. It was pretty rotten stuff … You know, I went for a walk about a month ago, and it took me down a bit of the Manifold. Anyway, I'm walking along this road – as wide as this – and, bugger me, there's a couple of limestone cliffs there with some blokes with pegs and climbing ropes on it!…' [DISSOLVES INTO MIRTH] '… My instinctive reaction to it was … *what for!?…*' [FURTHER LAUGHTER]

What, it looked silly to you, did it?

'Yeah! … yeah …' [STILL CHUCKLING]

Arthur Birtwistle in conversation, 1997

▶ 'Pulpit Ridge', a serious Hard VS on the Ravenstones above the Chew Valley, first climbed by Arthur Birtwistle in 1938. In the same year he made two very bold first ascents in Snowdonia which represented the absolute high point of British rock-climbing before the Second World War

Climber: Steve Dean

VJ DAY, 1945: BRAVE NEW WORLD

The atomic bomb on Nagasaki, and the Japanese surrender a few days later, ushered in an entirely new world in which everything was changed irreversibly. The war had been the great equalizer. The enterprise-stifling class structure which had handicapped Britain for so long, was now showing the first signs of breaking down. Following their victory over Hitler, the masses would no longer accept it as their lot to be second-class citizens. With full employment and rising wages as an unlikely bonus of war, and prospects under the new, Labour government of a greater distribution of wealth and even of a National Health Service, there was a new confidence in the air.

More importantly, for the people living in and around the Peak, the new government was committed to freedom of access to 'mountain, moorland, and rough grazing', a concept that had been repeatedly quashed by Tory majorities ever since the first attempt at an 'Access to Mountains Bill' in 1888. The government was also united in its belief that 'National Parks, so long talked about, must be brought into being'.

And now, on this 'VJ day', the very day that the Japs surrendered, we are back at Stanage in the company of two young lads from Sheffield: Albert Shutt, a school-leaver and Tom Probert, a fitter for English Steel. Tom, a 'tall, jovial sort of lad' was a strong climber who had already made a reputation with his friends for leading 'Cave Innominate' in the Lake District in bad conditions. Let Albert Shutt take up the story:

'Because it was VJ Day we got two days off. We went to Stanage because we hadn't got enough money to go anywhere else. We put a rope down "Left Unconquerable" to see if we could get up it. A lot of people had tried it. We spent the whole of the Saturday on it, and had lots of tries. I fell off every time, but by the end Tom could do it on a rope. On the last three or four times he got up it, and had worked out how to do the moves.'

In the evening they went back down to Hathersage to join the VJ celebrations, and returned many hours later, rather the worse for wear, to spend the night in Robin Hood's Cave.

The next day, August 16, dawned fine, and while the new rock ace of the time, Peter Harding, was doing a route at Black Rocks which he was to call appropriately 'VJ Crack', the modest Stanage team were making climbing history. Apparently they had made no plans whatever the evening before, but at first light, as they were getting up, Tom turned to Albert and said: 'Do you know, I think I can do that thing' – meaning, of course, the 'Left Unconquerable'. And he proceeded to lead it, straight off, on the first attempt, with absolutely no protection for there was none to be had. 'He was, of course, a fool,' says Albert, 'but a competent fool!'

Albert, who had had no luck the day before, now managed it, but only on a very tight rope. Flushed with success, they put a rope down the 'Right Unconquerable' but, perhaps rather surprisingly in view of his obvious ability, Tom could make no impression on it, falling repeatedly from the first really committing layback moves. When he eventually managed it, it was only on a very tight rope. How tight? 'I've still got scars to prove it!' says Albert.

Shortly afterwards Tom Probert joined the Navy and was never heard of again in the climbing world, but his climb was undoubtedly the most physically exacting pitch in Britain to date, and a fitting overture to the new age of climbing that was about to commence.

◄ 'The Left Unconquerable', the first to yield of a notorious pair of cracks at Stanage which had resisted all attempts ever since they were first tried (and named) by Eric Byne in 1932

Climbers: Steve Dean and Tim James

Peter Harding was the leading pioneer on Peak rock immediately after the War. His 'Promontory Traverse' (E1) at Black Rocks in 1945 and 'Suicide Wall' (HVS) at Cratcliffe in 1946 were indicative of a new level of ability; but he was also responsible for a number of all-time classic VS's such as 'Valkyrie' at the Roaches (shown here) and 'Phoenix' at Shining Clough (overleaf).

▲ Peter Harding on 'Valkyrie' at the Roaches in 1995, 49 years after making the first ascent

◀◀ Steve Dean in the same position on 'Valkyrie', just beyond the crux

▶ Peter Harding completing 'Valkyrie'

▶▶ The start and finish of Peter Harding's superb 'Phoenix Climb' at Shining Clough

Climbers: Dave Whitley and Keith Ashton

Many tales are told of climbers bold
Who perished in the snow
But this is a rhyme of the rise to fame
Of a working lad named Joe.
He came from good old Manchester
That quaint, old-fashioned town
And his name became a legend—
The legend of Joe Brown.

He first laid hand upon a crag
In the year of forty-nine,
He'd nowt but pluck, beginner's luck
And his mother's washing line.

Tom Patey, *The Joe Brown Song*, 1967

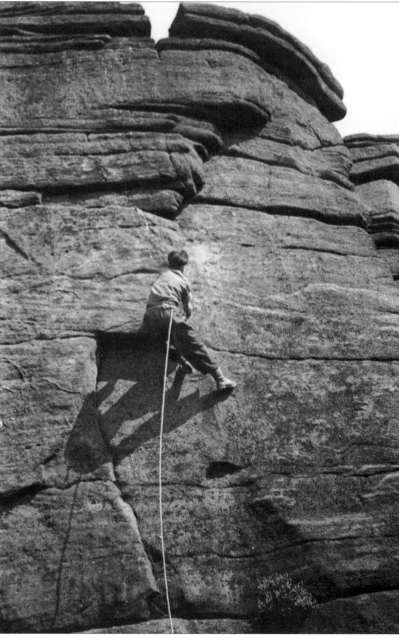

FIRST ASCENT OF 'THE RIGHT UNCONQUERABLE'

We now move on to a momentous day at Stanage in April 1949. Rumours have been circulating for a while of an extraordinary new climbing prodigy by the name of Joe Brown, and now we find him tying onto a hemp rope at the foot of the famous 'Unconquerables'. The onlookers watch in amazement as the 18-year-old Joe, knowing nothing of Probert's 1945 ascent, sets straight off up the 'Left Unconquerable' in his bendy plimsolls (above). But this is merely a preamble. Ernie Phillips' original, uncut roll of film goes straight from Wilf White seconding the route, also apparently with ease, to Joe standing on the first ledge of the 'Right Unconquerable'.

On the right is Ernie's famous photograph of the decisive moment as Joe launches into the first committing layback moves, an image that was to inspire a generation.

A previously unpublished frame (far right) shows Joe at the crux finishing moves with the rope hanging free from his waist without a single runner.

Joe does not recall having any trouble with the finish. 'Mantelshelves were something I was good at. I was a mass of muscle in those days.'

All photos: Ernest Phillips

47 years after making the first ascent of 'The Right Unconquerable', Joe Brown is back ...

Suddenly you go, swinging right up on to the flake, huge layback holds, hooked hands, the crack sometimes closing, occasioning little shuffles rightwards ...

Joe once again launching into the first committing layback moves on 'The Right Unconquerable', Stanage Edge, September, 1996. Belayed by Claude Davies

… awkward hand-changes, anxious moments … a race against failing strength and breath, fighting all the way, serious, yet an absolute joy in movement.

Jim Perrin

'The Right Unconquerable' rapidly became established as one of the all-time classic pitches of its grade, having for a while much the same status in the Peak as 'Cenotaph Corner' in North Wales (which Joe made the first ascent of in 1952).

'It was Wilf White who introduced us to Froggatt Edge near Sheffield. He went into raptures about fantastic walls and slabs of rough gritstone. "All blank, they are, and nobody has touched them".'

Joe Brown

'We were climbing on Froggatt in 1948 in tricounis, and just not quite making it, if you know what I mean. Because only the Valkyrie Club – Joe Brown and his mates - had the technique and the guts to go out onto those walls. We had looked at Froggatt Pinnacle. It seemed very hard. We tried it, but never got anywhere.'

R A (Dick) Brown

'After patiently watching the abortive efforts of our best men, Joe amazed the gathering by pulverising the oblique crack that splits the lower wall of the pinnacle, finally reaching the ledge in what we have all come to accept as the Joe Brown style.'

Nat Allen

▶ The crux of 'Valkyrie' (HVS) on Froggatt Pinnacle, another great classic climbed by Joe Brown just before he went into National Service in the summer of 1949

Climbers: Chris Thorp and Stuart Brooks

▼ A climber on the final slabby rib of 'Valkyrie', above the crux

Shortly after coming out of National Service in the spring of 1951, Joe Brown met up with Don Whillans (nickname 'the Villain'), who like himself was a plumber's apprentice. Together they were to form one of the strongest teams in the history of British climbing. Don Whillans was a very powerful climber who was capable of soloing 'Right Unconquerable' in suede shoes, and Peter Harding's desperate test piece, 'Demon Rib' (E2 5c) at Black Rocks, in big Austrian mountain boots.

In January 1953 they were staying in a barn below the Roaches …

'"Hey, how about having a go at the big overhang?" Joe Brown said suddenly.

"What now? In this?" The snow was drifting down quite thickly.

"Why not? It'll be dry under the overhang," he said.

… There was a whole mob of people around and as soon as they found out what we were going to do, they followed us up to the crag.

We tossed for who was going to lead and I won, much to Joe's disappointment.

… He took a stance on top of the Pedestal, sixty feet up and about fifteen feet below the overhang.

"Big, isn't it?" said Joe grinning.

"If I come off that I'll dinge myself a bit," I remarked.'

Eric Byne, an eye witness, recalled:

'The climber's position was now completely Sloth-like. Incredible as it may seem, he now moved outwards and upwards over the lip of the overhang entirely by hand jamming!'

'… By this time I was committed. I jammed my way along the crack until only the heel of my foot remained in the flake … Right. I reached out over the lip of the overhang for a hold above it and my foot came off the flake. I was hanging free from the tip of the overhang. I quickly pulled up, jammed a foot in the crack, whipped a runner on in case anything unaccountable happened, and pulled over the overhang. I was up.'

Tom Waghorn recalls: 'He dangled from the lip to show how easy it's done.'

◄ 'The Sloth' at the Roaches, on a fine evening in July. The buttress taken by 'Valkyrie' may be seen bottom right, while in the background is the miniature 'peak' of Hen Cloud

Climber: Kevin Anderson

The advanced hand-jamming techniques that Brown and Whillans developed at crags such as Curbar and Hen Cloud paid enormous dividends in the Alps, where they achieved international fame with rapid free ascents of, for example, the West Face of the Blaitière and the West Face of the Dru in 1954. Of the latter Joe commented: 'We really bombed up the face, pitch after pitch, without faltering.'

Joe Brown's 'Delstree' at Hen Cloud, so called because a delicate traverse is followed by a strenuous crack. It has been described by Jim Perrin as the best HVS south of Scotland

Climber: Steve Dean

▶ The strenuous part of 'Delstree', a superlative combination of bridging and jamming

Climber: Pete George

Here, on the great gleaming limestone crags of the dales, lies the future climbing ground of this country. Here are buttresses galore; great cliffs of incredible steepness and exposure that for years have attracted the admiring eyes of cragsmen. It is true, of course, that the stability of the rock is not above suspicion, but an examination of the great faces and bulges of rock that appear too smooth to climb shows that such rock is sound, steep and contains many infinitesimal finger holds, and that there lies the way.

Eric Byne's prophetic remarks in 1958

Ravensdale in late October

'Via Vita was the last of the obvious lines, and no one else was trying it. I was utterly and completely psyched up for it. I'd decided at the beginning of the year to do it in September.

'We did it in mountain boots – vibrams, not PA types. I could climb as hard in mountain boots as in PA's on small holds on limestone.

'I got onto that little hanging ledge, and inserted a chockstone in the back. There were just two other items of protection on the whole pitch: a thread before the swing to the right and a peg at the bottom of the final crack – driven upwards behind a flake. It remained there for years. It was one of the few pegs we bought – in Courmayeur in Italy. I was a metallurgist, so I normally made the pegs myself. (I was working three shifts on the furnaces at the steel works, and made blades and square channels out of bullet-proof steel.) I didn't use étriers or any aid at all. The only aid I used was hanging on the peg to clear out the crack which was choked with dirt and little chockstones. I cleaned it on the way up. I fell off about three times, but I knew that if I could get a hand jam I could get up.'

John Loy, 1996

▶ 'Via Vita' (HVS) in Ravensdale, first climbed by John Loy and Dave Mellor in September 1960, was a very advanced route for its date, being one of the hardest free climbs yet done on limestone. Cressbrook Mill lies just behind the wooded ridge in the background, where child apprentices once risked the very dangerous pastime of birdnesting (see Chapter 7)

Climber: Steve Dean

A rockclimber's apocalyptic vision of the wasteland, it is perhaps fitting that it attracts devotees of the ferocious, steep and uncompromising.

Paul Nunn's guidebook description of Stoney Middleton, 1975

Chris Jackson on his route 'Armageddon' (E2 5c, originally graded VS) at Stoney Middleton, which he first climbed in 1964

Geoff Birtles, one of the leading activists at Stoney Middleton in the mid-60s, had spotted the line of 'Armageddon', but made the mistake of telling his friend Chris Jackson about it, who went back and did it the following weekend. 'We had all became hooked on new routes,' says Geoff, 'and were very competitive in a friendly way. It was a very special, very exciting group of people. There was also the sense that Stoney Middleton was *ours*.'

A very fit Chris Jackson in 1996

Geoff Birtles remembers Chris Jackson in the '60s as being 'not very athletic and slightly overweight, but he had great vision.' The outstanding example of that vision was undoubtedly 'Debauchery', the stupendous free climb he made across the main face of High Tor in 1965 with John Atkinson. Up to that time this had been the domain of the peg-climber, and no one had even contemplated a free route, let alone tried it. 'There was absolutely no one else around,' says Jackson. 'We didn't know what to expect so we took a peg hammer and some pegs, but no étriers. It was just an adventure.' To their surprise they found a profusion of small pocket holds, and managed the whole route with just one peg for aid and an exciting pendulum on the first pitch. 'We just fought our way across it in about five hours.' Today there are many much harder climbs on the face, all of the highest quality and with an extraordinary degree of exposure. Tiptoeing in space above the everyday world of Matlock Bath, this is perhaps the ultimate 'Peak experience'. On first reaching the tree at the end of that giddy traverse I felt for a moment like Blondin, having crossed the Niagara Falls on a tightrope.

◄ Mind games in space. Chris Jackson at the crux of 'Debauchery'

► The crux of 'Debauchery' completed, Chris Jackson relishes the exposure above the Derwent at Matlock

'Bel Ami' (VS), Curbar Edge,
April 1969
Climber: John Stainforth

1968: THE TIMES THEY WERE A-CHANGIN'…

My brother, John, is seen here climbing in textbook fashion at Curbar Edge in 1969, as prescribed by the leading climbing manual of the day (dating from about 1965). He is using no runners at all, has a hawser-laid nylon rope attached with a shock-absorbing 'Tarbuck' knot and heavy steel karabiner to a hemp waistline, and is wearing excruciatingly uncomfortable (and unsticky) climbing boots (not to mention climbing breeches and a Norwegian oiled-wool sweater). But these were revolutionary times, and almost within months all this would change with the advent of infinitely superior 'kernmantel' ropes, climbing harnesses, much stickier boots, friction belay plates and the first commercially available, purpose-built 'nuts' for protection.

A man of his times: John Lumb (nickname 'Little John') on 'Friction Addiction' at Dovestones Crag in the Chew Valley

John Lumb has vivid memories, when starting to climb in the Chew Valley in '68, of bivvying alone in the cave on Dovestones Edge, which was known to climbers as the 'Dovestones Hotel', and watching, 'to the sound of the purring of the stove, the glow of a living city flickering to the west'. Or, on another occasion, of 'bounding down the steep peat at dusk to catch last beers at the Clogger's Arms'.

One of the larger-than-life characters in the Peak District in the late '60s and early '70s was Richard McHardy, famous for his bold soloing, and the inevitable string of serious injuries. Now one of the safest climbers around – and raconteur extraordinary – he is seen here leading 'The Hanging Crack' at Dovestones Edge thirty years after making the first free ascent in 1967. (The route had first been climbed some ten years previously by Joe Brown, using some aid.) On this occasion, as in 1967, Richard was belayed by his long-standing climbing partner Paul 'Tut' Braithwaite, himself an all-round mountaineer of vast experience.

▶ 'The Hanging Crack' (E2) at Dovestones Edge. After a gymnastic start the difficulties begin in earnest: a fierce crack narrows progressively until at the crucial point on the lip it will no longer accept ordinary hand jams

Sculptural rock formations at Dovestones Edge

▶▶ Richard McHardy on two superb limestone E1s in the southern Peak District: 'Lime Street Direct' at Willersley Castle Rocks and 'George' at Tissington Spires in Dovedale, both originally free-climbed at the very end of the sixties

With the advent of new, more sophisticated protection and belaying devices in the early 1970s, most limestone climbs that had previously required some aid were climbed free, so that quite suddenly there was a whole new style of climbing in the Peak to complement the already well established gritstone excellence. Crags such as Beeston Tor or Wild Cat Tor rapidly became popular alternatives to the old haunts of Stanage and Froggatt. And for the really 'far out' experience there was always 'Sirplum' in Chee Dale …

The superbly pocketed limestone of Beeston Tor on a fine summer weekend. Climbers can be seen on 'The Thorn', 'Pocket Symphony' and 'Deaf Dove'

'It was just another big, unclimbed wall. When I started up it I thought it might be an aid route. Because it was so overhanging we did no prior gardening. There was tons of loose rock on it. I put pegs in for protection and for resting on while I pulled off the loose rock. I had a bunch of about fifteen ex-WD and Cassin soft pegs, and one stainless steel peg which I put in the bedding plane above the first bulge. And I used one peg as a handhold to get up to the thread. None of my slings was long enough to go round the thread so I reversed to the peg and knotted two slings together, tying a fisherman's with one hand.

'From the thread it was entirely free. I went horizontally left to a big foothold and pulled straight up the big blocks above. I went like a bat out of hell. I got on one big brass nut – a plumbing fitting – for protection, and just carried on. It was still leaning. I got into a little groove capped by an overhang and managed to get on some small nuts. Then I got into the final finishing groove, where there were some good runners. The grass at the top was bloody terrifying – I was shoving my fingers into it and pulling up on grass sods. Then it was whoopee time!'

Bob Dearman, in 1998, remembering the first ascent of 'Sirplum' in the autumn of 1964

◀ Classic VS climbing at Wild Cat Tor in a beautiful woodland setting directly above Arkwright's Masson Mill on the River Derwent.
Left, 'Golden Yardstick', looking suitably golden on a fine October evening. Right, the excellent 'Cataclysm', first climbed in 1963 by Steve Read and Doug Scott (who, with Dougal Haston, was to be the first Briton to reach the summit of Everest in 1975)

Climbers: Chris Thorp and John Pereira

▶ At the thread on 'Sirplum' (E1 5b), one of the most sensational pitches of its standard in Britain

Climbers: Pete Rowlands and Joe Bawden

Despite the exciting developments on limestone in the early 1970s, gritstone remained the ultimate proving ground for sheer technical difficulty. Masters of the craft such as John Allen and Steve Bancroft pushed standards forward dramatically for the first time since the 'Brown era'.

◀ John Allen having little problem with gravity on his route 'Moon Walk' (E4 6a) at Curbar Edge, which he first climbed in 1975 with Steve Bancroft

▶ John Allen soloing another of his routes at Curbar, the exquisite mini-classic 'Fidget' (E1)

THE 1980s

Climbing changed dramatically in the 1980's with increased levels of training on indoor climbing walls and the advent of climbing competitions in 1989. Local Peak man, Simon Nadin, seen here hanging bat-like from the roof of Thor's Cave, was the first overall World Cup champion. But both he and Fliss Butler, seen opposite on Ilam Rock – herself three-times British Women's champion – are all-rounders who embody the best traditions of British 'adventure' climbing. They both say that they are happiest making on-sight ascents of good natural lines on outdoor crags.

Before the arrival of the Danes, Thor's Cave in the Manifold valley was associated with the local god, Hob, and later with the Green Man himself. Here, Simon Nadin, the 'Buxton Stick Man', is seen flitting up 'Thormen's Moth', Andy Pollitt's incredible free route out of the cave, first done as a difficult peg climb by Bob Dearman in 1969

'The White Edge' (E4 6a),
Ilam Rock, Dovedale

Climbers: Fliss Butler
and Ruth Jenkins

Ilam Rock in Dovedale was first climbed in 1903 by the alpinist Samuel Taylor who managed to throw a rope over the top and then shin up it hand over hand, watched by a large crowd. The first free ascent was made by the great Siegfried Herford on 'a dismal wet day' in August 1914 just before the Great War. It was probably one of the very last climbs that he made. The loose and dangerous route that he took on the far side has seldom been repeated; and the lurid account given by his companion, A R Thomson, of hanging to 'tufts of grass' and 'great pieces of rock that came off at a touch', did much to discourage limestone climbing for many years. The route shown here, 'The White Edge', was first climbed free in 1978 by the phenomenally powerful Ron Fawcett, of whom it was once said that if you cut through him it would spell rock.

'BODY MACHINE'

First climbed by Ron Fawcett in May 1984, this very difficult route on Raven Tor is regarded by the few who can do it as one of the best pitches of its type in the Peak. Yet many today remain uneasy about this new type of climbing. To many purists it seems to be a worrying departure from the essence of the game, and indicative of a new, consumerist approach which has no concern for either history or surroundings. This is an essentially more contrived game, of following entirely unobvious lines, using bolts or pegs for protection, without shame or restraint, and with little respect for the natural environment. The name 'Body Machine' neatly sums up the sheer reductionism of this new enterprise which turns climbing, as Johnny Dawes puts it, into little more than 'hard physical tasks'.

Sitting in my camera-seat about twenty feet out in space to take this photograph, I was struck by two things. First, Fliss's extraordinary ability to link together a sustained series of apparently inadequate 'holds'; and, secondly, just how unattractive the challenge looked at close quarters. Wherever I looked I could see shining bolts, rotting slings and rusty pegs. May it not perhaps seem to future generations – as indoor climbing-walls get better and better – to be an embarrassing folly, a tawdry, crumbling monument, like the Albert Memorial, to a bygone age? A fitting reminder, perhaps, of the shallowest, most materialistic and self-centred decade since the time of the Romans? So that in addition to the Greek term *Hubris* (the name of another climb hereabouts), we may perhaps recall those grim old Latin words: *Damnati in metalla*.

And how many climbers who come here ever take any interest in that other crumbling monument, the ruin of Litton Mill, the relic of child slavery that lies just a few hundred yards downstream?

▶ Fliss Butler on 'Body Machine'

Nijinsky. A little madman, a little clown, gambolling about on the carpet in unutterable, elastic glee. Don't send him grey hairs too soon, you Roman Gods! Don't gripe too hard, you fellow-men. This is Brown in his youth, self-possessed of his huge talent.

Jim Perrin on Johnny Dawes

MIND OVER MATTER

In 1984 a new star, by the name of Johnny Dawes, burst on the climbing firmament with a brilliance and an energy not seen since Joe Brown's startling debut in 1948. Not only had no one ever seen anybody climb quite like this before – he rapidly gained an awesome reputation for being able to 'pull on dots and rock over on a hyphen' – but most of his new routes were of a boldness and a blankness that they had never seriously been considered as climbing possibilities. Technical masterpieces like 'Braille Trail', 'End of the Affair' and 'Gaia' pointed the way far into the future. (The exquisite 'Gaia', E8, at Black Rocks has only been led four times in eleven years, and another frightener, 'White Lines' at Curbar Edge, still awaits a second ascent.)

On a fine June evening in 1995, high above the upper reaches of the Derwent, which have already played such an important part in the Peak history books, we find Johnny preparing to add yet more dots and hyphens to its pages. This activity, which may seem to the outsider to be utterly detached from all that has gone before, is yet rooted in the same tradition of boldness and defiance that has always found a home among these abrasive, magical rocks …

▶ Attempting to climb a new line over the biggest overhang at Bamford Edge

Climbers: Shane Ohly and Johnny Dawes

After several attempts on the new line, Johnny manages to top rope it. He comes bounding down the path.

'OK, I'm going to solo it!'

'Don't you think you should use a rope?' I ask nervously, certain types of news photography quite definitely not being my forte.

'Oh, OK then' – and within moments Shane Ohly is tending the ropes on the half-way ledge and Johnny is chalking up. He gives me so little time that I simply stick the camera on a tripod directly below the climb to show the full extent of the roof, which is beautifully lit now in the evening sun.

There is a pause while Johnny arranges the first and only runners.

Then suddenly he is away …

He climbs the route so fast that, without a motordrive on my Hasselblad, I have time only to take four frames, the first and last of which are shown here. The sense of will-power as he explodes upwards in a series of precise and rapid movements is almost palpable. There is not the slightest doubt that he is going to get up it. It's the nearest thing I've ever seen to a pure demonstration of mind over matter.

Later, in the pub, Johnny enthuses about the 'best pinch' he's ever come across – 'a leafy pinch on the lip which fills the hand. Beyond that there's a flat sloper. Once you've learnt the moves, it's just as easy to shut the eyes – it's very easy to do it right!'

His intellect rushes on, like his climbing, in leaps and bounds:

'All life comes from earth … When we actually subdue our own thoughts to rock, we find out that we've got something very similar within us. It brings us to a universal state that is very difficult to inhabit in any other way. I mean, it doesn't excite you, it *embeds* you. It's a different thing – it *grounds* you.'

Yes, but most of us it grounds in a rather different way.

Johnny Dawes making the first
ascent of 'Avoiding the Traitors'
(E7 6c), Bamford Edge
26 June 1995

An 'appointment with fear' on The Prow at Wimberry Rocks

◄ The view, directly below The Prow, of the Chew Plantation and Dovestone Reservoir on a fine midsummer evening

The aptly named 'Appointment with fear' (E7 6b), first climbed by Dougie Hall in 1986, involves a desperately precarious series of balance moves on minute pebbles. The very serious consequences of a fall from this exposed position on the arête are only too obvious. Sam Whittaker, one of the emergent aces of the present generation, said it was one of the most exhilarating and exposed routes he'd ever done.

Leo Houlding, a new
wunderkind in the Dawes
mould, soloing Peter Harding's
great test piece, 'Demon Rib'
at Black Rocks (E3 5c), on
sight at the age of 16

THE FUTURE

The rock of the Peak District continues to reveal an apparently
inexhaustible supply of climbing riches. Some of the longest
used crags such as Black Rocks at Cromford, which encapsulates
the whole history of Peak Climbing, are still capable of producing
magnificent surprises. As this book was nearing completion, one
of the greatest remaining challenges on gritstone, the
preposterously smooth and holdless front of the Promontory,
which had taunted generations as an 'impossible possibility',
was at last led in magnificent style by Seb Grieve. Gently
overhanging in its lower half, with a series of exceptionally
tenuous moves above an appalling landing, and with no
protection at all until the main difficulties are over at 35 feet,
this is currently the most daunting undertaking in the Peak.

The name of the climb, 'Meshuga', is Hebrew for 'crazy', and
so by a strange coincidence this brief resumé of Peak District
climbing starts and finishes with a crazy pinnacle. But perhaps
it is not so strange, if this book is seen as being, among other
things, a history of craziness.

▶ This classic problem,
'Oedipus! Ring Your Mother'
on Froggatt Pinnacle (E4 6b),
was first climbed in 1968 by
Tom Proctor, the leading
climber in the Peak before the
appearance of John Allen.
Stuart Brooks is seen here
making a bold attempt which
came within inches of success,
before he executed an equally
impressive controlled descent
and leap to safety

▶ Seb Grieve on the final moves of his 'state-of-the-art' gritstone masterpiece 'Meshuga' (E9 6c) at Black Rocks. This final section was first climbed as long ago as 1949 by Peter Harding as a provocatively named 'Easy Exit' to his own famous 'Promontory Traverse' (E1) of 1945

Dyno for the scoop, heel hook, cross for the edge, hand on the arête, foot on the arête, foot flag, slap up, got the pocket, knee in the scoop, pocket, pocket, break, arête, break, Friend 1, big smile.

Seb Grieve's description of the first ascent of 'Meshuga', November 1997

Pull
up on jugs of gritstone. Crimp
on folds of compressed sand. File
movement smooth in mind. Touch

rough quartz studs. Fashion
delicate pain in ornate thoughts. Jam
soft flesh fists tight in cracks. Sculpt
in the medium of wind-carved flakes and overlaps. Balance

desires on sharp arêtes ...

From *Craft*, by Mark Goodwin

◄ Getting to grips with
'Rainbow Crack' (VS 5a) on
Hen Cloud
Climber: Chris Thorp

185

Rob's Rocks, Chew Valley
Climber: John Lumb

We reached the first stragglers of the battalion of rocks … where the mountain shook off turf and flower, had only heath for raiment and crag for gem – where it exaggerated the wild to the savage, and exchanged the fresh for the frowning – where it guarded the forlorn hope of solitude, and a last refuge for silence.

Charlotte Brontë, *Jane Eyre*

▶ The Nose, Rob's Rocks

◀ 'East Rib' (HVS 5a),
Shining Clough

Climber: Steve Dean

What a still, hot, perfect day! What a golden desert this spreading moor!
Everywhere sunshine. I wished I could live in it and on it. I saw a lizard run
over the crag; I saw a bee busy among the sweet bilberries.

Charlotte Brontë, *Jane Eyre*

Boulder field below Shining
Clough, Longdendale

The Rivelin Needle,
attractively situated above the
Rivelin Reservoir less than two
miles from the outskirts of
Sheffield, was named by J W
Puttrell, who tried it without
success in about 1890. Sixty
years were to pass before
Donald Wooller and Dick
Brown managed to climb it
without aid. In 1953 they came
back and did this route on the
front face which they called
'Croton Oil', after a drastic
tropical purgative, for reasons
that are best not elaborated

Climbers: Chris Thorp
and Peter Roberts

… a more empty, homeless scene you cannot find. It is a fitting region for creatures that love loneliness; and you have them near. The curlew calls plaintively across the marshy cloughs. The gun-surviving hawk sails past on easy wing scanning the great hillsides, and the plover wails from the fields that edge the moor below. A hare, startled from amid the rocks, darts off in a straight line, trusting only to its speed, terrified by the unusual sight of man. It is a wild, wide place, far from the ways of men, who here are the most occasional of creatures, and all its notes have the sadness of great spaces — of the mountains, moors, and seas. And yet it does one good to get into this upland, age-long solitude, where the primeval world is felt to be a mighty fact, linked to us.

G H B Ward, 1934

◄ 'Jester Cracks' (VS), Ashop Edge, high above Ashop Clough, Kinder Scout

Climber: Steve Dean

◄ On Alderman's Rocks above the Chew Valley, the scene of a stupendous boulder-throwing contest between the legendary giants Alphin and Alderman

Climber: John Lumb

The immaculate, beautiful, but blandly named 'Boulder Climb' on Robin Hood's Stride was compared in difficulty on its first ascent in 1897 by the legendary Owen Glynne Jones with the crux pitch of the mighty Dent du Géant in the French Alps. This was once, after all, the home of the Derbyshire giant, Hob

Climber: John Cutcliffe

9 Ghosts

REMINDERS OF THE PAST

We like to think of the Peak National Park, scarcely two generations old, as something very permanent, as if it has always been here and will continue to be like this into the foreseeable future. The fact that the landscape has changed out of all recognition even in the last hundred years, and could easily do so again, is not an idea that we are glad to entertain. But when the great reservoirs of the Upper Derwent – which have been such an attractive addition to the Peak landscape – run dry, and the mud-cloaked stumps of Derwent village are exposed again for all to see, they are an ugly and disturbing reminder to us of the transience of history. And yet some ghoulish fascination compels us to take a look, to see for ourselves this real 'skeleton in the cupboard' of recent history, for we know that, for all our technical wizardry, we cannot free ourselves completely from the burdens of the past. And as we enter the new, much-trumpeted 'Age of Aquarius', and fleets of water-tankers urgently ferry water back and forth by road in a forlorn bid to outweigh our own greed and wastefulness, many such ghosts remain …

◀ The Ladybower Reservoir in March 1995 …

▶ … and eight months later, with the remains of Derwent village exposed

Howden Reservoir, the site of medieval Ronksley ('Proud Man's Clearing'), on a cold evening in November

▶ Looking south over Howden Reservoir from Ronksley Moor. In late medieval times, all the land on the right (west) bank of the Derwent was within the Royal Forest of the Peak, while that on the left was Hallamshire. Derwent Abbey lay just beyond the left end of the dam. Directly beyond that, on the skyline, is Win Hill

'THE LAND OF THE RUSH'

Up until the last century, the steep hill slope below the Roaches, once called Anu's Rocks, would echo to shouts and laughter on the evening of Beltaine (May 1) as the people rolled large *cakes* into the so-called 'Custard Field' – just as in days of old they had rolled 'wheels of fire' (probably barrels of flaming tar) down the hill in honour of Anu, the earth mother, and Bel, the supreme God of Light (father of Lu, the sun god). For many centuries these old pagan gods were never far away, and in the middle ages, in the days of the White Monks, this land above the Abbey of Dieulacres was known not only as the 'Roches' but as the 'Land of the Rush'; for frequently an angry rush of wind would come tearing down the slope from the 'Windygates' beside Hern's Cloud, as demons tried yet again to claim the body of the nobleman who had founded the Abbey. The monks now called Bel 'Beelzebub', Baal-Zebul, the 'lord of the flies'.

In more recent times there are still occasional reports of people being knocked down by 'the rush'.

▶ Dusk falls on Tittesworth Reservoir below the Roaches in early June

Nescitis horam; Vigilate; Orate – You know not the hour; watch; pray

Inscription on one of the graves of the plague victims of Eyam, 1666

Yeoman Hay Reservoir and Dovestones Edge, Chew Valley, at dusk

As the night closes in we begin to hear strange and indeterminate sounds, which may or may not be distant animal cries. In the half-light, our eyes start to play tricks and we may even fancy that we can see the phantom lights of Saddleworth Moor ... It was, of course, on a night such as this in the early 1960s that a notorious pair of sadistic murderers were out on the moor above Standing Stones disposing of their victims ... And what part did the phantom lights play when a local MP, out walking on Ashway Moss in the 1850s, accidentally turned his gun on himself?

► Yeoman Hay Reservoir and Alderman Brow, Chew Valley

Primitive man is here, buried no one knows how long ago, on these remote hill-top fastnesses; and our own people, naming things with names we still understand, have been here these thousand years or more; but from first to last, man counts for but little in these wastes; the listening hills, and homeless winds, and streams, laughing as they ceaselessly delve their deepening channels, are the main enduring facts.

GHB Ward, 1934

On a night such as this, as dusk draws in on the crags, perhaps we might even hear the voices of the pioneer climbers in their old haunts under Kelly's Overhang and Jeffcoat's Buttress. But will we listen to their story?

▶ Ramshaw Rocks on a very cold evening in December

◄ The ravine of Kyndwr Scut retreats into the depths of the night

… Perhaps they are all out tonight: the ghosts of the Brigantes at Arbor Low, waving their phantom axes, the Roman legion on Bleaklow, the phantom huntsman of Bretton Clough with his Gabriel Hounds, the cowled monk of Cratcliffe under the yew trees at Robin Hood's Stride, the grey ladies of Nine Stones and Bamford Edge dancing to the sound of fairy pipes, the crazy woman of the Roaches conversing with the creature of Doxey Pool – and all those other headless women and horsemen: of Matlock Moor, Earl Sterndale and Ashover, Butterton Moor and the Woodhead Pass. And skulking in the darkness, the black dogs of Barmoor Clough and Edale, and lurking in the ravine below the Downfall, the dreaded 'Kinder Boggart'. Perhaps they will always be here.

NOTES

p.10 *The People of the Heights.* The Celtic name *Brigantes*, referring to the confederation of tribes occupying the entire Pennine area of England, meant just this.

p.21 *The Wanderers*: the seven planets, including the sun and moon, in distinction to the 'fixed stars' (from Gr. *planes*, wanderer).

p.29 *The standing stones of Arbor Low.* One theory has it that the stones were never in an upright position; and the Nine Stones were definitely left intact by the Romans: there were seven still standing in 1829. Sadly, today there are only four.

p.26 *Enormous men with big feet … Roman 'miles'.* The average height of a Roman man was 5' 7". A Roman foot was about 11.6 present-day inches, and about one Roman inch (*uncia*) longer than the 'megalithic' foot (1 'megalithic yard' being equal to 2.72 present feet). A Roman (double) 'pace' equalled 5 Roman feet, and a Roman mile was a 1000 of these (*mille passus*).

p.35 *German invaders … bigger feet.* The English foot was nearly half an inch longer than the Roman. See note to p.26, above.

p.36 *The Ram in the thicket, Bull in the thorn.* I suggest the phenomenon that we now call the 'precession of the equinoxes', in which the 'First Point of Aries' has moved over the last 4000 years from Taurus, through Aries and Pisces, to Aquarius, is at least one possible signification of the Bull i' th' Thorn, Hob in the Hurst, and Ram in the thicket motif which is reflected in some Derbyshire place-names. A hostelry called 'The Bull' was established at Hurdlow Thorn in 1472. There is a carving on a wood panel inside, dating from 1642, showing the bull entangled in the thorn bush.

p.38 *Edwin … hanged … from a tree.* The tree, known successively as Edwin's Tree, Edden's tree, and Eden tree, was somewhere in the region of the present Eden Tree campsite and the New Bath Hotel at Bradwell.

p.49 *Henry II … wore a sprig of broom in his hat.* Whence the House of Plantagenet got its name (broom = *genista*). The full Derby coat of arms also features a ram stepping between two sprigs of broom.

p.50 *The Arwey to Matlac.* The old Roman 'Army Way' (see Ch 2, p.29), called successively through the Middle Ages: Arwey, Hareway, Herwardstrete, and Hereward Street.

p.68 *Robin Hood depicted as having ram's horns.* Interestingly, in France the word 'Robin' came to mean both the 'devil' and a 'ram'; and Pennethorne Hughes has suggested that the word 'fairy' may be derived from the Latin *fera*, 'a wild animal'.

p.76 *Hobbes' 'Seven Wonders of the Peak'* – a house, a mountain, a chasm, two fountains and two caves – were: Chatsworth, Mam Tor, Eldon Hole, St Anne's Well (Buxton), the Ebbing-and-Flowing Well (Barmoor Clough), Poole's Cavern (Buxton), and Peak Cavern (Castleton).

p.84 *The old Celtic injunction against cutting down oaks* (see Ch.1, p.15). As recently as September 1997, Derby quarry workers refused to cut down an old oak tree, where a witch was said to be buried, through fear of a fatal curse.

p.84 *The magnate … who could move mountains.* For example, in 1702 the 1st Duke of Devonshire removed a hill at Chatsworth where the 'Canal Pond' now stands, opening up the view to the south. Eventually, in 1843, even mock outcrops would be created in the gardens, in incongruous proximity to the fine natural crag of Chatsworth Edge just around the corner.

p.87 *Hobbyhorse.* Note that the words Hob, Hobgoblin, Hoby, Hobyn, Hobin, Robyn, and Robin, are all etymologically and mythologically very closely related.

p.99 *Narrow bridges … were frequently swept away.* For example, Calver Bridge in 'the great flood' of August 1799, and Mytham Bridge at Bamford in 1856.

Some Hob place-names in and around the Peak (with O.S. grid references):

Hob Hall, Wirksworth SK 288527
Hob Hill, Hazlewood SK 328460
Hob Lane, near the Robin Hood Inn, Holmesfield SK 316782
Hob Lane, Kirk Ireton SK 275498
Hob Hurst's House, Hartland Edge, Beeley Moor SK 287693
Hob Hurst's House (= Thor's Cave) SK 098549
Hob Tor, near Dove Holes SK 063773
Hob Wood, Wirksworth SK 287525
Hobb Stones, Wharncliffe SK 307954
Hob Holme, north of old Derwent Village
Hobroyd Farm, near Glossop SK 028931
Hob's House (= Hob Thirst Hole), Monsal Dale SK 175712
(Hob) Thurst House Cave, Deep Dale SK 097712 (1417)

Some Robin Hood place-names in and around the Peak and Sherwood (dates of the first known reference in brackets):

Little John's Grave, Hathersage churchyard SK 231815 (1680)
Little John's Well, Longshaw Estate SK 267794
Hood Brook, Hathersage SK 230835
Robin Hood's Bower, Greno Wood, Sheffield SK 332945 (1637)
Robin Hood's Cave, near Annesley, Sherwood SK 510544 (1700)
Robin Hood's Cave, Creswell Crags SK 535743
Robin Hood's Cave, Stanage SK 244836
Robin Hood's Chair, Hope Dale SK 213820 (referred to in 1882)
Robin Hood's Chair, Robin Hood Hills, Sherwood SK 516546
Robin Hood Close, Nottingham (1485 *Robynhood Closse*)
Robin Hood's Croft, above Ladybower Reservoir, Lead Hill SK 197867
Robin Hood Cross, Bradwell Edge SK 183803 (1319, *Robin Crosse*)
Robin Hood's Cross, Pleasley SK 504642
Robin Hood Farm, near Calverton, Sherwood SK 582494 (1840)
Robin Hood's Grave, near Creswell Crags SK 540730 (1840 *Robins Grave*)
Robin Hood Hamlet and Inn, near Baslow SK 280721 (1824 *Robin Head*)
Robin Hood Hamlet, near Whatstandwell SK 332551
Robin Hood Hill and Pit, near Oxton, Sherwood SK 635538 (1825)
Robin Hood's Hills, near Annesley, Sherwood SK 515547 (1775)
Robin Hood Inn, Lidgate, west of Holmesfield SK 308778 (1820)
Robin Hood Inn, Stannington, near Loxley, Sheffield SK 307891
Robin Hood's Larder, a large tree in Sherwood Forest (which survived until the late 1950s) where Robin Hood was said to have hung venison. SK 607676
Robin Hood's Leap, Chatsworth Park
Robin Hood Moss, Howden Moors SK 190930
Robin Hood's Picking Rods, Rowarth SK 006909 (1842)
Robin Hood's Piss Pot, near Blidworth, Sherwood SK 610536
Robin Hood's Spring, Howden Moors SK 193933
Robin Hood's Stable, Papplewick, Sherwood. A cave cut into sandstone. SK 548517 (Probably a Victorian invention)
Robin Hood's Stone, near Newstead Abbey, Sherwood SK 544541
Robin Hood's Stoop, Offerton Moor SK 217807 (a very ancient boundary stone)
Robin Hood's Stride, Harthill Moor SK 223623 (1790 *Robin Hood's Strides*, in John Byng's 'Tour of the Midlands')
Robin Hood's Table, Barbrook Valley SK 277755 (Probably named after the 6th Duke of Rutland who was nicknamed Robin Hood and had shooting parties here in 1860s)
Robin Hood's Tree, Wharncliffe Crags. No longer in existence.
Robin Hood's Well, near Beauvale Priory, Sherwood SK 497491
Robin Hood's Well, Longshaw Estate SK 267799 (1809)
Robin Hood Well, Low Hall Wood, Sheffield SK 333965 (1773)
Robin Hood's Well, Monk Wood, south of Dronfield SK 349764
Robin Hood's (or St Anne's) Well, Nottingham SK 589419 (1500 *Robynhode Well*, 1551 *Seynt Anne Well*)
Robin Hood's Whetstone, near Clipstone SK 604623

Nicknames and unusual pronunciations:

Alderwasley *ALLERSLOE*
Ashover *ASHER*
Bolsover *BOWSER*
Bonsall *BONSER*
Bradwell *BRADDER*
Calver *CARVER*
Crich *CRIGHTCH*
Derby *DARRAND* (apparently commonly used in the 18th century)
Edensor *ENSOR* or *ENZER*
Eyam *EEM*
Lose Hill *LOOSE HILL* (One theory has it that the name means 'pigsty hill')
Onecote *ONCUT*
Pindale *PINDER*
The Portway near Monsal Head (aka. Castlegate) *SCRATTER*
Smalldale *SMAWDER*
Tideswell *TIDZEL, TIDSER*; and the inhabitants, *TIDSERITES*
Tintwistle *TINSEL*
Wirksworth *WOOSER* or *WUZZER*
Youlgreave *POMMY* (from the sound of the village's first brass band which marched around playing 'Pom-pom-pom!')

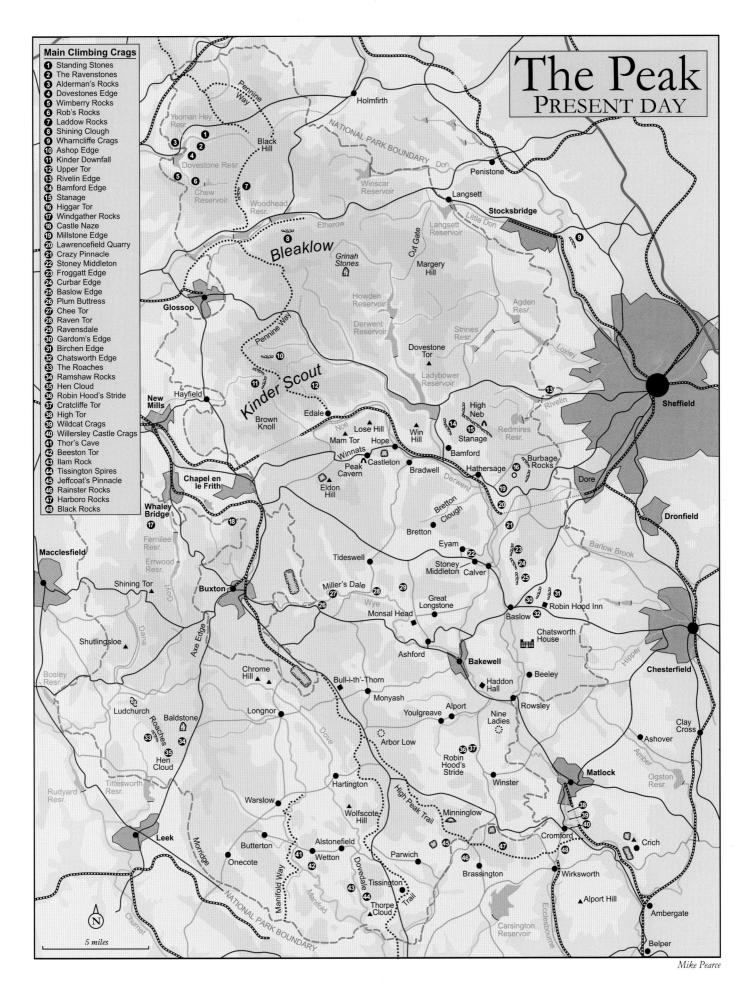

Main Climbing Crags

1. Standing Stones
2. The Ravenstones
3. Alderman's Rocks
4. Dovestones Edge
5. Wimberry Rocks
6. Rob's Rocks
7. Laddow Rocks
8. Shining Clough
9. Wharncliffe Crags
10. Ashop Edge
11. Kinder Downfall
12. Upper Tor
13. Rivelin Edge
14. Bamford Edge
15. Stanage
16. Higgar Tor
17. Windgather Rocks
18. Castle Naze
19. Millstone Edge
20. Lawrencefield Quarry
21. Crazy Pinnacle
22. Stoney Middleton
23. Froggatt Edge
24. Curbar Edge
25. Baslow Edge
26. Plum Buttress
27. Chee Tor
28. Raven Tor
29. Ravensdale
30. Gardom's Edge
31. Birchen Edge
32. Chatsworth Edge
33. The Roaches
34. Ramshaw Rocks
35. Hen Cloud
36. Robin Hood's Stride
37. Cratcliffe Tor
38. High Tor
39. Wildcat Crags
40. Willersley Castle Crags
41. Thor's Cave
42. Beeston Tor
43. Ilam Rock
44. Tissington Spires
45. Jeffcoat's Pinnacle
46. Rainster Rocks
47. Harboro Rocks
48. Black Rocks

The Peak
PRESENT DAY

Mike Pearce

PHOTOGRAPHIC NOTES

As with my previous books many subjects were photographed that were not eventually used. Much very publishable material had to be rejected because it did not finally suit the flow of the story or the requirements of the design, or because there was simply not enough space in what was already a very large book. From Laddow and Ludchurch to Beeston Tor and Birchen Edge many painful exclusions had to be made; I was particularly sorry to debar material that had cost much effort in more esoteric locations such as Gradbach, The Hanging Stone, Far Black Clough, Harston Rock, Bosley Cloud, Shell Brook and Greasley Hollow. Many of the limestone dales suffered a similar fate, from Cave Dale, Monk's Dale, and Deep Dale in the north to Lathkill Dale, Gratton Dale, Long Dale, and the Hamps Valley in the south.

As with many professional photographers, I regularly update my camera kit, so that not all the cameras listed below were owned by me at any one time during this two and a half year shoot. The Fuji GSW690, for example, was replaced by the Horseman SW612 for the widest angle climbing shots. In addition, equipment occasionally had to be hired for specific projects, such as the 500mm lens for the moonrise at Robin Hood's Stride.

The Hasselblad remains my 'workhorse' camera for standard landscape work. The other cameras are used specifically for double-page spreads, or for climbing shots taken by hanging from a static rope. For the latter a typical kit will consist of my Sekonic spotmeter, the SW612 with the 6 x 9 back (which takes only 8 frames and is impossible to reload when dangling from a rope), the Fuji 645 (which takes 15 frames), and sometimes also the Fuji 690. Because I am thus very heavily laden I use a wooden sit-seat in addition to a climbing harness, and move up and down the rope using Petzl ascenders and a Petzl 'Stop'.

All the images in the book, apart from four shots involving later 'digital manipulation' – the carriage wheel on page 73, the monks on horseback at Nine Stones Circle on pages 52 and 53 (in which the number of riders was increased) and 'The Sloth' on page 144 (in which distracting background spectators were removed) – are single exposures involving no modification of any kind, and minimal filtering.

CAMERAS

Blad	Hasselblad 500 C/M 6x6cm roll film SLR camera
GW	Fuji GW690II 6x9cm roll film rangefinder camera
GSW	Fuji GSW690III 6x9cm roll film rangefinder camera
SW	Horseman Super Wide 612 6x12cm camera with 6x9 roll film back
GA	Fuji GA645 Professional 6x4.5cm autofocus camera

LENSES

500mm	Zeiss Tele-Apotessar CF 500mm F8
150mm	Zeiss Sonnar CF 150mm F4
90mm	EBC Fujinon 90mm F3.5 (on Fuji GW690)
80mm	Zeiss Planar CF 80mm F2.8
65mm	EBC Fujinon 65mm F5.6 (on Fuji GSW690)
60mm	Super EBC Fujinon 60mm F4 (on Fuji GA645)
50mm	Zeiss Distagon CF 50mm F4
45mm	Rodenstock Apo-Grandagon 45mm F4.5
TC	Teleplus MC6 2 x Teleconvertor

FILMS

RDP	Fujichrome 100D Professional 120
RDPII	Fujichrome Provia 100 Professional 120
RAP	Fujichrome Astia 100 Professional 120
RHP	Fujichrome Provia 400 Professional 120
PRZ	Kodak Panther 100X 120
RKR	Kodachrome Professional 64 120

FILTERS

SL	Skylight (1A or 1B) filter
UV	Ultraviolet filter
81A	Light amber filter
Grad	Graduated ND filter (2 stops)
Pol	Polarizer

EXPOSURE METER

Sekonic Dual Spot F L-778

OTHER SYMBOLS

+1, +2	Pushed one, or two, stops
↵	Shot involved single rope techniques (i.e. hanging from a rope)

Cover	Parkhouse Hill and Chrome Hill	2.30 pm	Late Feb	GW	90mm	f16	1/250	81A	RDPII
Page 1	Dovedale in the autumn	1.45 pm	Mid-Nov	Blad	150mm	f8	1/125	81A	RDPII
2-3	'Baldstone Arête'	2.15 pm	Early Aug	GSW	65mm	f11	1/250	81A	RDPII
4-5	'Moyer's Buttress', Gardom's Edge	2.30 pm	Late Oct	GSW	65mm	f5.6	1/60	81A	RDPII
6	Climbing on Harboro Rocks	5.45 pm	Late Mar	Blad	50mm	f4	1/125	UV	RDPII
7	Harboro Rocks at sunset	6.00 pm	Mid-Oct	GA	60mm	f5.6	1/125	81A	RDPII
8	'The Winking Man', Ramshaw Rocks	10.45 am	Mid-Nov	Blad	50mm	f8	1/125	Pol	RDPII
9	Stars over Rainster	12.20 am	Early May	Blad	50mm	f5.6	7 mins	None	RDPII
10	Nine Ladies Stone Circle	7.00 pm	Mid-Apr	Blad	80mm	f19	1/8	SL	RDPII
11	Sunset over Mam Tor	6.00 pm	Mid-Oct	Blad	50mm	f6.8	1/250	None	RDP
12	Woodland below Gardom's Edge	3.35 pm	Early Nov	Blad	150mm	f4	1/125	81A	RDPII
13	Thorpe Cloud and River Dove, winter	12.15 pm	Late Jan	Blad	50mm	f16	1/60	UV	RDPII
14	Roystone Rocks	5.15 pm	Late Feb	Blad	50mm	f5.6	1/60	UV	RDPII
14	Rowan tree berries	3.30 pm	Late Nov	Blad	150mm	f11	1/30	81A	RHP
15	Dead rowan tree at Aldwark	6.30 pm	Mid-Oct	Blad	150mm	f9.5	1/8	81A	RDPII
16	Bamford Edge in mist	10.10 am	Mid-Sept	Blad	150mm	f13.5	1/60	81A	RDPII
17	Ramshaw Rocks	11.45 am	Early May	Blad	50mm	f11	1/125	UV	RDPII
17	Rosebay Willowherb in Chee Dale	5.40 pm	Mid-Oct	Blad	80mm	f4.8	1/4	SL	RDPII
18	Sunset from Robin Hood's Stride	9.10 pm	Mid-July	Blad	500mm	f11	1/250	None	RHP
19	Moonrise over Thorpe Cloud	9.10 pm	Mid-May	Blad	150mm	f4.8	1/4	None	RDPII
20	Moonrise at Robin Hood's Stride	9.30 pm	Mid-July	Blad	500mm	f9.5	1/15	None	RHP
21	Comet Hale-Bopp over Minninglow	10.45 pm	Mid-Apr	Blad	80mm	f2.8 (+ 2)	27 secs	None	RHP
22	Minninglow from Roystone Rocks	5.40 pm	Late Feb	Blad	50mm	f6.8	1/15	UV	RDPII
28	Mam Tor in winter	2.15 pm	Early Feb	Blad	50mm	f19	1/125	UV	RDPII
29	Rowan branch below Birchen Edge	4.15 pm	Late Oct	Blad	80mm	f6.8	1/125	UV	RDPII
30	Carsington Reservoir	6.30 am	Early Jun	GW	90mm	f9.5	1/60	81A	RDPII
31	Minninglow at sunset	6.45 pm	Early Oct	Blad	150mm	f4.8	1/125	81A	RDPII
32-3	Bonsall Moor in winter	11.30 am	Late Nov	GW	90mm	f13.5	1/250	81A	PKR
34	Chrome Hill in winter	1.30 pm	Late Dec	Blad	50mm	f16	1/250	UV	RDPII
37	Bretton Clough in the mist	11.45 am	Mid-Oct	Blad	80mm	f13.5	1/125	SL	RDPII
39	Sunset on Win Hill	6.00 pm	Mid-Oct	Blad	80mm	f11	1/125	None	RDP
40-1	Five Clouds below the Roaches	7.30 pm	Early Aug	Blad	50mm	f4.8	1/500	UV	RDPII
42-3	Mermaid's Pool, Kinder Scout	7.30 pm	Early Apr	Blad	50mm	f5.6	1/125	UV	PRZ
44	The Dove Valley from Pilsbury	4.45 pm	Mid-Oct	Blad	150mm	f9.5	1/60	81A	RDPII
46	Peak Cavern	5.15 pm	Mid-Mar	Blad	50mm	f4.8	1/125	UV	RDPII
47	Woods below Beeley Moor	11.15 am	Mid-Nov	Blad	150mm	f13.5	1/60	81A	RDPII
48-9	Beeley Moor at sunset	3.50 pm	Mid-Nov	Blad	150mm	f4.8	1/60	81A	RDPII
50-1	Ronksley Valley in winter	2.30 pm	Late Nov	Blad	50mm	f9.5	1/125	UV	RDPII
52	Monks passing Nine Stones Circle	10.45 am	Mid-Dec	Blad	80 x 2	f5.6	1/125	SL	RDPII
53	Monks passing Nine Stones Circle	11.15 am	Mid-Dec	Blad	150mm	f6.8	1/125	81A	RDPII
55	Abbey Brook	3.55 pm	Late Nov	Blad	80mm	f5.6	1/4	SL	RDPII
58-9	Dovedale in the autumn	2.50 pm	Mid-Nov	GW	90mm	f4.8	1/15	81A	RDPII
60-1	Woodland below Gardom's Edge	2.45 pm	Early Nov	GSW	65mm	f8	1/250	81A	RDPII
62	Woodland beside Padley Gorge	3.05 pm	Mid-Nov	Blad	150mm	f4.8	1/500	81A	RDPII
64	Hob's House, Monsal Dale	2.00 pm	Late Oct	Blad	150mm	f9.5	1/125	81A	RAP
65	Ashop Clough in winter	5.15 pm	Early Mar	Blad	50mm	f11	1/125	UV	RDP
66-7	Mist over the Padley Gorge	11.10 am	Mid-Oct	Blad	150mm	f32	1/30	Grad	RDPII
68	Monsal Dale in the evening	3.20 pm	Late Oct	Blad	150mm	f8	1/30	81A	RAP
70	Chatsworth Park in the autumn	2.30 pm	Mid-Nov	Blad	150mm	f4.8	1/250	81A	RDPII
74	Carriage on the Old Portway	2.30 pm	Early Oct	Blad	150mm	f8	1/125	81A	RDPII
76	'Daniel Defoe and acquaintance'	3.30 pm	Early Oct	Blad	150mm	f4.8	1/125	81A	RHP
76	'Defoe in the carriage'	2.30 pm	Early Oct	Blad	80mm	f8	1/125	SL	RDPII

77	'Defoe' looking out of carriage	2.30 pm	Early Oct	Blad	150mm	f8	1/125	81A	RDPII
77	The River Derwent and High Tor	3.00 pm	Mid-July	Blad	50mm	f9.5	1/125	UV	RDPII
78-9	High Tor in the evening sun	3.30 pm	Late Nov	Blad	150mm	f4.8	1/125	81A	RDPII
80	Carriage on Beeley Moor	2.00 pm	Early Oct	GW	90mm	f9.5	1/125	81A	RDPII
81	Carriage above Chatsworth Park	2.30 pm	Early Oct	Blad	50mm	f11	1/125	UV	RDPII
82-3	Chatsworth, South Wing	9.30 am	Mid-Nov	Blad	150+TC	f9.5	1/15	81A	RDP
85	Felled oak in Chatsworth Park	1.45 pm	Late Nov	Blad	150mm	f19	1/30	81A	RDPII
86-7	Chatsworth Park from Hunting Tower	8.15 pm	Late May	SW	45mm	f11	1/8	81A	RDPII
88	Weir in Monsal Dale	2.30 pm	Late Oct	Blad	150mm	f32	1/2	81A	RDP
91	Icy wall on Rowlee Pasture	11.45 am	Late Jan	Blad	50mm	f16	1/125	UV	RDPII
92	The ruin of Litton Mill	6.15 pm	Late July	GA	60mm	f5.6	1/90	81A	RDPII
94	The pool at Water-cum-Jolly	11.00 am	Mid-Nov	Blad	150mm	f16	1/15	81A	RDPII
97	Winnats Pass in winter	1.10 pm	Early Feb	Blad	80mm	f11	1/250	SL	RDPII
98	Looking down into Winnats Pass	5.00 pm	Early Feb	Blad	80mm	f8	1/15	SL	RDPII
99	The Matterhorn Ridge, Winnats Pass	1.45 pm	Early Feb	Blad	80mm	f9.5	1/250	SL	RDPII
100	Snake Pass in winter	11.15 am	Late Jan	Blad	50mm	f19	1/250	UV	RDPII
102-3	Monsal Viaduct, Monsal Dale	2.35 pm	Late Oct	Blad	150mm	f27	1/8	81A	RAP
104	Robin Hood's Quarry	4.45 pm	Early May	Blad	150mm	f8	1/8	81A	RDPII
105	Mossy rock in Duke's Quarry	4.15 pm	Early May	Blad	150mm	f8	1/30	81A	RDPII
106	Edensor, Chatsworth Park	9.50 am	Mid-Nov	Blad	150mm	f8	1/125	81A	RDPII
108	'Puttrell's Progress', Wharncliffe	4.30 pm	Early Apr	Blad	50mm	f9.5	1/125	UV	RDPII
109	'The Crazy Pinnacle'	2.30 pm	Mid-Nov	Blad	50mm	f9.5	1/125	UV	RDPII
110	Hen Cloud at sunset	8.15 pm	Early May	Blad	150mm	f4.8	1/125	81A	RDPII
110-11	'The Arête', Hen Cloud	2.15 pm	Early Nov	GSW	65mm	f11	1/125	81A	RHP
113	'Jeffcoat's Pinnacle'	4.00 pm	Early Apr	Blad	80mm	f5.6	1/125	SL	RDPII
114-15	'Sand Buttress', Black Rocks	7.30 pm	Early Sept	SW	45mm	f13.5 (+2)	1/125	81A	RDPII ⏎
116-17	'Kelly's Overhang', Stanage	7.15 pm	Early June	GW	90mm	f8	1/60	81A	RDPII
119	'Tower Face', Wharncliffe	11.30 am	Early Apr	Blad	50mm	f6.8	1/125	UV	RDPII
120-1	'Cave Gully Wall', Stanage	8.30 pm	Late July	GSW	65mm	f9.5	1/125	81A	RDPII
122	'Elliott's Buttress Direct', Gardom's	11.45 am	Mid-Oct	GA	60mm	f6.8	1/125	81A	RDPII
123	Windy Buttress, Stoney Middleton	3.00 pm	Early Oct	GA	60mm	f6.8	1/90	81A	RDPII
124	Kinder Scout from Hollin Head	1.50 pm	Early Feb	Blad	50mm	f11	1/250	UV	RDPII
125	Kinder Downfall in winter	2.40 pm	Early Feb	Blad	50mm	f16	1/250	UV	RDPII
126	'Upper Tor Wall', Grindsbrook	1.45 pm	Early Apr	Blad	80mm	f13.5	1/125	SL	RDPII
127	Arthur Birtwistle, Grindsbrook	11.45 am	Early Nov	Blad	80mm	f8	1/250	SL	RDPII
129	'Pulpit Ridge', Ravenstones	6.30 pm	Late June	GA	60mm	f8	1/90	81A	RDPII ⏎
130	'Left Unconquerable', Stanage	11.30 am	Early June	Blad	80mm	f9.5	1/250	SL	RDPII
132-3	'Valkyrie' at the Roaches	11.30 am	Early Aug	GSW	65mm	f9.5	1/250	81A	RDPII ⏎
134	Peter Harding on 'Valkyrie', Roaches	8.15 pm	Mid-July	GA	60mm	f6.8	1/125	81A	RDPII ⏎
134	Peter Harding	8.45 pm	Mid-July	Blad	150mm	f8	1/125	81A	RDPII
135	Peter Harding finishing 'Valkyrie'	8.30 pm	Mid-July	Blad	150mm	f9.5	1/125	81A	RDPII
136	'Phoenix Climb', Shining Clough	11.50 am	Late June	GA	60mm	f9.5	1/180	81A	RDPII
137	'Phoenix Climb', Shining Clough	11.30 am	Late June	Blad	150mm	f6.8	1/500	81A	RDPII
140	Joe Brown on 'Right Unconquerable'	11.45 am	Early Sept	GA	60mm	f4.8	1/90	81A	RDPII ⏎
140	Joe Brown on 'Right Unconquerable'	11.45 am	Early Sept	GA	60mm	f4	1/250	81A	RDPII ⏎
141	Joe Brown on 'Right Unconquerable'	11.45 am	Early Sept	GA	60mm	f4	1/350	81A	RDPII ⏎
142	Froggatt Pinnacle	1.30 pm	Mid-Oct	GA	60mm	f11	1/125	81A	RDPII
143	The crux of 'Valkyrie', Froggatt	1.00 pm	Mid-Oct	Blad	150mm	f8	1/250	81A	RDPII
144	'Sloth', the Roaches	8.00 pm	Mid-July	GA	60mm	f8	1/90	81A	RDPII ⏎
146	Starting up 'Delstree', Hen Cloud	11.45 am	Mid-July	Blad	50mm	f11	1/125	UV	RDPII
147	'Delstree', Hen Cloud	6.00 pm	Mid-Sept	SW	45mm	f9.5 (+1)	1/125	81A	RDPII ⏎
148	Kath Pyke leading 'The Rasp'	1.00 pm	Mid-Aug	SW	45mm	f12.7	1/125	81A	RDPII ⏎

149	Joe Brown	3.45 pm	Early Sept	GA	60mm	f5.6	1/60	81A	RDPII
150-1	High Tor in winter	10.45 am	Mid-Mar	Blad	80mm	f4.8	1/125	SL	RDPII
152	Ravensdale	2.00 pm	Late Oct	Blad	80mm	f8	1/125	SL	RDPII
153	'Via Vita', Ravensdale	7.15 pm	Mid-Sept	GA	60mm	f4	1/90	81A	RDPII ↵
154-5	'Armageddon', Stoney Middleton	2.00 pm	Early Nov	SW	45mm	f9.5	1/250	81A	RHP ↵
156-7	'Debauchery', High Tor	2.30 pm	Late Oct	SW	45mm	f19	1/250	81A	RHP ↵
158	Chris Jackson	3.15 pm	Early Nov	Blad	150mm	f8	1/250	81A	RHP
159	Chris Jackson on 'Debauchery'	2.45 pm	Late Oct	GW	90mm	f19	1/250	81A	RHP
161	John Lumb at Dovestones Edge	5.00 pm	Mid-June	Blad	80mm	f5.6	1/125	SL	RDPII
162	Rock sculpture at Dovestones	3.15 pm	Mid-June	GA	60mm	f9.5	1/180	81A	RDPII
163	McHardy on 'The Hanging Crack'	4.45 pm	Mid-June	Blad	150mm	f4.8	1/250	81A	RDPII ↵
164	McHardy on 'Lime Street Direct'	5.15 pm	Mid-June	GA	60mm	f4.8	1/60	81A	RDPII ↵
165	'George', Dovedale	2.45 pm	Mid-Oct	Blad	50mm	f9.5	1/125	UV	RDPII
166	'Golden Yardstick', Wild Cat Tor	6.00 pm	Early Oct	GA	60mm	f6.8	1/125	81A	RDPII ↵
167	'Cataclysm', Wild Cat Tor	4.45 pm	Early Oct	GA	60mm	f5.6	1/125	81A	RDPII ↵
168	Beeston Tor	2.00 pm	Mid-Oct	Blad	150+TC	f5.6	1/125	81A	RDPII
169	'Sirplum', Chee Dale	7.45 pm	Early July	Blad	150mm	f9.5	1/500	81A	RHP ↵
170-1	John Allen on 'Moonwalk', Curbar	4.00 pm	Late Oct	GW	90mm	f13.5	1/125	81A	RHP
171	John Allen solos 'Fidget', Curbar	3.15 pm	Late Oct	GW	90mm	f8	1/125	81A	RDPII
172	'Thormen's Moth', Thor's Cave	1.00 pm	Early Aug	GA	60mm	f4.8	1/125	81A	RDPII
173	'The White Edge', Ilam Rock, Dovedale	12.45 pm	Late July	Blad	50mm	f9.5	1/125	UV	RDPII
174-5	Fliss Butler on 'Body Machine'	4.30 pm	Late July	SW	45mm	f8	1/125	81A	RDPII ↵
176	Johnny Dawes bouldering	7.15 pm	Mid-June	Blad	50mm	f9.5	1/125	UV	RDPII
177	Bamford Edge and Ladybower	9.00 pm	Mid-June	Blad	50mm	f9.5	1/125	UV	RDPII
178-9	'Avoiding the traitors', first ascent	8.45 pm	Mid-June	Blad	50mm	f8	1/125	UV	RDPII
178	'Avoiding the traitors', first ascent	8.45 pm	Mid-June	Blad	50mm	f8	1/125	UV	RDPII
180	Chew Plantation below Wimberry	8.45 pm	Early June	GA	60mm	f4	1/45	81A	RDPII
181	'Appointment with Fear', Wimberry	8.45 pm	Late June	GA	60mm	f4	1/60	81A	RDPII ↵
182	Leo Houlding solos 'Demon Rib'	3.30 pm	Late June	GA	60mm	f11	1/180	81A	RDPII
182	'Oedipus, Ring your mother', Froggatt	12.30 pm	Late Oct	GA	60mm	f11	1/125	81A	RDPII
183	Seb Grieve on 'Meshuga', Black Rocks	12.30 pm	Mid-Feb	Blad	80mm	f5.6	1/250	UV	RHP
184-5	'Rainbow Crack', Hen Cloud	11.45 am	Early Nov	GSW	65mm	f5.6	1/125	81A	RHP
186	Rob's Rocks, Chew Valley	5.00 pm	Mid-June	GA	60mm	f8	1/125	81A	RDPII
187	The Nose, Rob's Rocks	5.15 pm	Mid-June	GA	60mm	f8	1/90	81A	RDPII
188	'East Rib', Shining Clough	11.15 am	Late June	GA	60mm	f9.5	1/125	81A	RDPII
189	Boulders below Shining Clough	12.30 pm	Late June	GA	60mm	f8	1/125	81A	RDPII
190	'Croton Oil', Rivelin Needle	11.30 am	Mid-June	GA	60mm	f9.5	1/125	81A	RDPII
191	Rivelin Needle and Rivelin Reservoir	11.30 pm	Mid-June	GA	60mm	f9.5	1/125	81A	RDPII
192-3	'Jester Cracks', Ashop Edge	2.00 pm	Mid-July	GW	90mm	f8	1/125	81A	RDPII
194	'Great Slab Arete', Alderman's Rocks	11.45 am	Mid-June	GA	60mm	f11	1/180	81A	RDPII
195	'Boulder Climb', Robin Hood's Stride	6.00 pm	Early Apr	Blad	50mm	f9.5	1/125	UV	RDPII
196	Ladybower Reservoir in winter	11.35 am	Late Mar	Blad	80mm	f11	1/500	SL	PRZ
197	Ladybower Reservoir in a drought	1.30 pm	Late Nov	Blad	50mm	f8	1/125	UV	RHP
198	Howden Reservoir	3.00 pm	Late Nov	Blad	80mm	f13.5	1/15	SL	RDPII
199	Howden Reservoir from Ronksley Moor	2.15 pm	Late Nov	Blad	150mm	f9.5	1/125	81A	RDPII
200-1	Tittesworth Reservoir at dusk	8.50 pm	Early June	Blad	150mm	f6.8	1/125	UV	RDPII
202	Yeoman Hay reservoir at dusk	9.30 pm	Mid-June	GA	60mm	f4.8	1/60	81A	RDPII
203	Yeoman Hay reservoir at dusk	9.15 pm	Mid-June	GA	60mm	f5.6	1/90	81A	RDPII
204-5	Ramshaw Rocks at dusk	4.00 pm	Early Dec	Blad	150mm	f11	1/4	81A	RDPII
206	Nightfall on Kinder Downfall	5.15 pm	Early Feb	Blad	80mm	f5.6	1/8	SL	RDPII
207	Moonrise over Thorpe Cloud	9.10 pm	Mid-May	Blad	150mm	f4.8	1/4	None	RDPII
Rear jkt	Johnny Dawes at Robin Hood's Stride	7.30 pm	Early Apr	Blad	50mm	f5.6	1/125	UV	RDPII

BIBLIOGRAPHY

GENERAL

WILLIAM ADAM, *Gem of the Peak*, Longman, London, 1838
Of great historical interest, and wonderfully evocative.

JOHN BARNATT and KEN SMITH, *Peak District: Landscapes through time*, Batsford, London, 1997
A very thorough survey of different aspects of Peak archaeology, marred only by some curiously arcane maps.

JULIE BUNTING, *A Peakland ABeCedary*, J. H. Hall, Derby, 1993

K. CAMERON, *The Place-names of Derbyshire* (3 Vols), Cambridge University Press, 1959
The standard work, with a particularly interesting introduction.

F. WOLVERSON COPE, *Geology Explained in the Peak District*, David & Charles, Newton Abbot, 1976

ELIZABETH EISENBERG, *The Derbyshire Year*, J. H. Hall, Derby, 1989

J. B. FIRTH, *Highways and Byways in Derbyshire*, Macmillan, London, 1908
One of the best books on Derbyshire ever produced, beautifully written, exquisitely illustrated, and clearly the source material for many subsequent books.

RAY MANLEY and ROLAND SMITH, *Time Exposure*, Peak Park Joint Planning Board, Bakewell, 1991

ARTHUR MEE, *Derbyshire*, Hodder & Stoughton, London, 1937
A quaint curate's egg of a book, more concerned with churches and tombs of the gentry than with landscape or social history.

A. D. MILLS, *Oxford Dictionary of English Place Names*, Oxford University Press, 1991

PATRICK MONKHOUSE, *On Foot in the Peak*, Maclehose, London, 1932
A lyrical classic by a Peak devotee.

LINDSEY PORTER, *The Peak District: its secrets and curiosities*, Moorland Publishing, Ashbourne, 1988

ROGER A. REDFERN, *A Picture of the Peak District*, Robert Hale, London, 1987
Written by a walker with an exceptional grasp of local history.

LES ROBSON, *A Gazetteer of the White Peak*, J. H. Hall, Derby, 1991

ROLAND SMITH, *First and Last: The Peak National Park*, Peak Park Joint Planning Board, Bakewell, 1978
The best brief overview of the National Park in all its aspects.

MARTIN SPRAY, *Peak District Place Names*, JNM Publications, Matlock, 1989

HISTORY: GENERAL

JULIE BUNTING, *A Peakland Chronology*, J. H. Hall, Derby, 1994
—— *The Earls and Dukes of Devonshire*, Footprint, Ripley, 1996

P. P. BURDETT, *A Map of Derbyshire*, 1791, Derbyshire Archaeological Survey, 1975

JOY CHILDS, *A History of Derbyshire*, Phillimore, Chicester, 1989
A good introduction to the whole span of local history; concise and very readable.

DAVID CLARKE, *Ghosts and Legends of the Peak District*, Jarrold, Norwich, 1991

A. E. DODD and F. M. DODD, *Peakland Roads and Trackways*, 2nd edn., Moorland Publishing, Ashbourne, 1980
A delightful and fascinating study which urgently needs to be reprinted.

JOHN HEATH, *An Illustrated History of Derbyshire*, Breedon Books, Derby, 1993
A very thorough work, with much interesting archive material.

JOHN N. MERRILL, *Legends of Derbyshire*, Dalesman Books, Clapham, 1972
—— *Derbyshire Folklore*, Footprint Press, Ripley, 1995

H. M. PARKER and L. WILLIES, *Peakland Lead Mines and Miners*, Moorland Publishing, Ashbourne, 1979

DOUG PICKFORD, *Magic, Myth and Memories of the Peak District*, Sigma, Wilmslow, 1993

CRICHTON PORTEOUS, *The Ancient Customs of Derbyshire*, Derbyshire Countryside, Derby, 1976

BRIAN ROBINSON (ed.), *The Seven Blunders of the Peak*, Scarthin Books, Cromford, 1994
A very varied collection of essays, debunking some long-cherished Peak myths, which ranges from the scholarly and balanced to the prejudiced and cynical.

LYNN WILLIES, *Lead and Leadmining*, Shire Publications, Princes Risborough, 1994

HISTORY: LOCAL

MAXWELL CRAVEN, *Derby: History and Guide*, Alan Sutton Publishing Ltd, Stroud, 1994

SETH EVANS, *Bradwell: Ancient and Modern*, Derbyshire Archaelogical Society, 1912

DORIS HOWE, *The Story of Holbrook*, Scarthin Books, Cromford, 1984

DOUG PICKFORD, *Staffordshire, Its Magic and Mystery*, Sigma, Wilmslow, 1994

RON SLACK, *Land and Lead-Miners: a history of Brassington*, Chesterfield, 1991

DEREK WAIN, *Whatstandwell*, Whatstandwell, 1995
Much interesting historical detail in all these.

CHAPTER 1: PREHISTORIC AND CELTIC

JOHN BARNATT, *Stone Circles of the Peak, A Search for Natural Harmony*, Turnstone Books, London, 1978 (now out of print)
A fascinating and expertly researched book, which succumbs in the final pages to a mystical and far-fetched theory that a 'Great Triangle' divides the Peak landscape into twelve equal parts that relate to the Zodiac. Recommended nevertheless.

AUBREY BURL, *Prehistoric Henges*, Shire Publications, Princes Risborough, 1991
—— *Prehistoric Stone Circles*, Shire Publications, Princes

Risborough, 1997

NORA CHADWICK, *The Celts*, Penguin Books, Harmondsworth, 1970

Still probably the best introduction.

PAUL DAVIES, *The Mind of God*, Simon & Schuster, London, 1992

A richly stimulating survey, by a scientist, of man's relation with the cosmos.

ROBERT GRAVES, *The White Goddess*, Faber & Faber, London, 1961

A unique, intensely learned study of the most ancient myths underpinning our culture.

D. B. GREGOR, *Celtic, a comparative study*, The Oleander Press, Cambridge, 1980

JOHN MICHELL, *The Earth Spirit: Its Ways, Shrines and Mysteries*, Thames & Hudson, London, 1975

PETER J NAYLOR, *Celtic Derbyshire*, J. H. Hall, Derby, 1983

GERDA and JOHN PICKIN, *Prehistoric Derbyshire*, J. H. Hall, Derby, 1984

STUART PIGGOTT, *The Druids*, Penguin Books, Harmondsworth, 1968

The standard work on the subject.

ALWYN REES and BRINLEY REES, *Celtic Heritage*, Thames & Hudson, London, 1961

An extraordinarily rich, scholarly book, rather more accessible than Graves. Particularly good on Celtic numerology.

ANNE ROSS, *Everyday Life of the Pagan Celts*, Batsford, London, 1970

A very well researched book by one of the leading scholars on the subject.

JOHN SHARKEY, *Celtic Mysteries, The Ancient Religion*, Thames & Hudson, London, 1975

An attractive and balanced overview, with a fine introduction.

CHAPTER 2: ROMAN

JOHN J. ANDERSON, *Roman Derbyshire*, J. H. Hall, Derby, 1985

MAURICE BRASSINGTON, *Roman Derby*, Breedon Books, Derby, 1991

PETER CONNOLLY, *The Roman Army*, Macdonald, London, 1975

EDWARD GIBBON, *The Decline and Fall of the Roman Empire*, ed. Dero A. Saunders, Viking Penguin, New York, 1980

HARRY LANE, *The Romans in Derbyshire: Lead mining and the search for Lutudarum*, Veritas Publications, Chesterfield, 1986

PETER SALWAY, *Roman Britain*, Clarendon Press, Oxford, 1981

CHAPTER 3: THE DARK AGES

RICHARD BUNTING, *Anglo-Saxon and Viking Derbyshire*, J. H. Hall, Derby, 1993

PENNETHORNE HUGHES, *Witchcraft*, Longmans, London, 1952

A wide-ranging and beautifully written masterpiece, both erudite and entertaining. Highly recommended.

JOHN MORRIS, *The Age of Arthur* (3 vols), Phillimore, London, 1977

The standard work on the early Dark Ages. Gigantic and labyrinthine, but of immense importance.

THEODORE ZELDIN, 'The Viking fear of being forgotten', in *An Intimate History of Humanity*, Harper Collins, London, 1994

Just one of many surprising gems in a rich and stimulating book.

PHILIP ZIEGLER, *The Black Death*, Collins, London, 1969

A fine book, but not much on the Peak District as such.

CHAPTER 4: THE ROYAL FOREST OF THE PEAK AND ROBIN HOOD

D. J. BRADBURY, *Secrets of Sherwood*, Mansfield, 1987

R. B. DOBSON and J. TAYLOR, *Rymes of Robyn Hood, An Introduction to the English Outlaw*, Heinemann, London, 1976

Contains the original texts of most of the Robin Hood ballads, including the *Gest of Robin Hood*. A very learned and authoritative introduction traces the whole development of the myth right up to the present day. Essential reading.

Hallamshire: A note on its meaning and the extent of the territory it represents, Department of Local History, Sheffield City Libraries, 1954

This brief pamphlet only goes some of the way towards unravelling a baffling subject.

J. C. HOLT, *Robin Hood*, Thames & Hudson, London, 1982; revised edn. 1989

The best single study of the Robin Hood legend. The postscript to the revised edition presents new historical evidence which puts the original Robin Hood firmly back in the early thirteenth century and renders much previous pseudo-scholarship obsolete.

MAURICE KEEN, *The Outlaws of Medieval Legend*, Routledge & Kegan Paul, London, 1961; Revised ed.1977

A classic and highly readable work, wide-ranging in its implications.

HENRY KIRKE, 'The King's Forest of the High Peak', *The Reliquary*, Vol VIII, 1867-8

I have found no modern study on the Royal Forest of the Peak to equal this. Pithy and evocative.

WILLIAM LANGLAND, *Piers the Ploughman*, trans. J. F. Goodridge, Penguin Books, Harmondsworth, 1959

JIM LEES, *The Quest for Robin Hood*, Temple Nostalgia Press, Nottingham, 1987

W. R. MITCHELL, *The Haunts of Robin Hood*, Clapham, 1970

GRAHAM PHILLIPS and MARTIN KEATMAN, *Robin Hood: The Man behind the Myth*, London, 1995

I mention this book only to warn that its case for a fourteenth-century 'original' Robin Hood in Wakefield has been completely scuppered by the findings of Professor Holt.

JOSEPH RITSON, *Robin Hood: a collection of all the ancient poems, songs and ballads*, London, 1795; Broomhead, Stockport, 1994

This classic, antique collection of ballads contains some which are not included in Dobson and Taylor.

SIMON SCHAMA, Ch 3: 'Liberties of the Greenwood', *Landscape and Memory*, Harper Collins, London, 1995

A study of our relation to landscape that is of unprecedented breadth and depth. Already a classic.

MICHAEL E. SMITH, *Derbyshire's Monastic Heritage*, J. H. Hall, Derby, 1985

—— *Castles and Manor Houses in and around Derbyshire*, J. H. Hall, Derby, 1992

ROLAND SMITH, 'Following the Steps of Robin Hood', *Peak Park News*, Summer 1976

Some useful local references.

CHARLES R. YOUNG, *The Royal Forests of Medieval England*, Leicester, 1979

A good general study, but rather thin on the Peak Forest.

CHAPTER 5: TUDOR AND STUART

JOY CHILDS, *Tudor Derbyshire*, J. H. Hall, Derby, 1985

ELIZABETH EISENBERG, *The Captive Queen in Derbyshire*, Footprint Press, Ripley, 1984

THOMAS HOBBES, *Leviathan*, London, 1651; ed. C. B. Macpherson, Penguin Books, Harmondsworth, 1968

An extraordinary classic by a fearless rationalist: vehement, witty, and astonishingly modern; with a fine introduction by Macpherson.

PENNETHORNE HUGHES, *Witchcraft*, Longmans, London, 1952. See comments under Chapter 3.

BRIAN STONE, *Derbyshire in the Civil War*, Scarthin Books, Cromford, 1992

A very interesting book as far as it goes, but there is clearly much work still to be done on the subject.

CHAPTER 6: THE AUGUSTAN AGE

STEPHEN DANIELS, 'The Political Iconography of Woodland in Later Georgian England', in *The Iconography of Landscape*, ed. Denis Cosgrove and Stephen Daniels, Cambridge University Press, 1988

An excellent essay, mercilessly modern (and consequently rather 'politically correct' in tone).

THE DUCHESS OF DEVONSHIRE, *Chatsworth Garden*, Derbyshire Countryside, Derby, 1996

—— *Chatsworth*, Derbyshire Countryside, Derby, 1997

DANIEL DEFOE, *A Tour through the Whole Island of Great Britain*, London, 1724-6; ed. Pat Rogers, Penguin Books, Harmondsworth, 1971

CELIA FIENNES, *Through England on a Side-Saddle*; 1685-1712; ed. Christopher Morris as *The Illustrated Journeys of Celia Fiennes*, Alan Sutton, London, 1982

SIMON SCHAMA, 'Hearts of Oak and Bulwarks of Liberty?' (in Ch 3) and 'Arcadia Redesigned' (Ch 9), in *Landscape and Memory*, Harper Collins, London, 1995

Even better here than he was with his discussion of Robin Hood. (See comments above.)

CHAPTER 7: INDUSTRIAL REVOLUTION

MAUREEN ALLEN, *Cressbrook*, Caldbeck, 1996

JULIE BUNTING, 'Give a man a good name', in *The Seven Blunders of the Peak*, ed. Brian Robinson, Scarthin Books, Cromford, 1994

A balanced and well argued reappraisal of William Newton, 'The Minstrel of the Peak'.

JOHN BYNG, VISCOUNT TORRINGTON, *Tour in the Midlands, 1790*, in *Rides Round Britain*, ed. D. Adamson, Folio Society, London, 1996

Provides a vivid glimpse into an almost unrecognizable world at the outset of the Industrial Revolution: tough, primitive, and claustrophobic. Essential reading.

THOMAS CARLYLE, *Signs of the Times*, London, 1829, in *Thomas Carlyle, Selected Writings*, ed. Alan Shelton, Penguin Books, Harmondsworth, 1971

BRIAN COOPER, *Transformation of a Valley*, Scarthin Books, Cromford, 1991

A detailed and superbly accomplished study of the impact of the Industrial Revolution on the Derwent valley. Highly recommended.

EDMUND AND RUTH FROW (ed.), *The Dark Satanic Mills, Child Apprentices in the Derbyshire Spinning Factories*, Working Class Library, Salford, 1980

Shattering first-hand accounts by two child apprentices (given in their old age) of conditions in Cressbrook Mill at the beginning of the nineteenth century.

VIC HALLAM, *Towers of Strength*, Chesterfield, 1991

An attractive and well illustrated account of the construction of the Howden, Derwent, and Ladybower Reservoirs.

G. M. TREVELYAN, *British History in the Nineteenth Century and After*, Longmans, London, 1937

JOHN RUSKIN, *The Stones of Venice*, Vol 2, Ch VI, London, 1867

—— *Fors Clavigera*, Vol 1, London, 1877

CHAPTER 8: HISTORY OF ROCK CLIMBING IN THE PEAK

1. BOOKS

ERNEST A. BAKER, *Moors, Moors, Crags and Caves of the High Peak and Neighbourhood*, Heywood, London, 1903

A classic. Superbly written, but structurally rather disorganised.

JOE BROWN, *The Hard Years*, Gollancz, London, 1967

A unpretentious modern classic by the leading climber of his age. The opening chapters on his upbringing in the Manchester slums and his first climbs are particularly vivid.

ERIC BYNE and GEOFFREY SUTTON, *High Peak*, Secker & Warburg, London, 1966

The standard (and only) work covering the early history of walking and climbing in the Peak. In serious need of updating with a supplement covering the last thirty years.

HOWARD HILL, *Freedom to Roam*, Moorland Publishing, Ashbourne, 1980

An important history of the struggle for access to Britain's hills. Very good on the Peak District.

GEOFF MILBURN (ed.), *On Peak Rock*, British Mountaineering Council, 1993

A superb summary of Peak District climbing, beautifully produced by a team of enthusiasts.

BERNARD NEWMAN (ed.), *Extreme Rock*, Diadem, London, 1985

PAUL NUNN, *Rock climbing in the Peak District*, Constable, London, 1975

A precursor of Milburn's book, with excellent black and white crag photographs by Tony Riley.

BENNY ROTHMAN, *The 1932 Kinder Trespass*, Willow Publishing, Altrincham, 1982

ROLAND SMITH, 'Forgive us our trespassers', in *The Seven Blunders of the Peak*, ed. Brian Robinson, Scarthin Books, Cromford, 1994

An interesting discussion of the Kinder Trespass which attempts to separate hard historical fact from pink-spectacled fiction.

DON WHILLANS and ALICK ORMEROD, *Portrait of a Mountaineer*, Heinemann, London, 1971

Not as fine a work as the Brown autobiography, but the authentic voice of Whillans nevertheless.

KEN WILSON (ed.), *Hard Rock*, Hart-Davis, Macgibbon, London, 1974

—— *Classic Rock*, Granada, London, 1978

2. SOME EARLY GUIDEBOOKS OF PARTICULAR HISTORICAL INTEREST

ALLAN ALLSOPP (ed.), *Climbs on Gritstone: Kinder, Roches and Northern Areas*, Willmer Bros, Birkenhead, 1951

ERIC BYNE (ed.), *Climbs on Gritstone: The Sheffield Area*, Willmer Bros, Birkenhead, 1951

Contains P. A. Barnes' photograph of Fred Pigott seconding the first ascent of Kelly's Overhang.

—— *Rock climbs in the Peak: The Sheffield – Stanage Area*, Cloister Press, Stockport, 1964

Contains P. A. Barnes' photograph of Morley Wood making the first ascent of Kelly's Overhang.

—— *Rock climbs in the Peak: The Saddleworth – Chew Area*, Cade and Co, London, 1965

—— *Rock climbs in the Peak: The Chatsworth – Cromford, Brassington Area*, Climbers' Club, Manchester, 1970

Contains particularly detailed historical notes.

FERGUS GRAHAM (ed.), *Recent Developments on Gritstone*, privately printed by Peak District climbing clubs, 1923

A real collector's item. Laycock's introduction is a classic in its own right.

P. R. J. HARDING and A. J. J. MOULAM, *Black Rocks and Cratcliffe Tor*, Climbers' Club, Manchester, 1949

JOHN LAYCOCK, *Some Gritstone Climbs*, Refuge Printing Department, Manchester, 1913

Another collector's item, deliciously succinct. Contains some historically very interesting photographs.

H. C. PARKER (ed.), *Climbs on Gritstone: Laddow Area*, Willmer Bros, Birkenhead, 1948

WILLIAM T. PARMER, *Odd Corners in Derbyshire*, Skeffington and Son, London, 1938

G. H. B. WARD, *Across the Derbyshire Moors*, 23rd edn., The Sheffield Telegraph and Star, 1946

A uniquely eloquent walkers' guidebook.

G. T. W. WEST, *Rock Climbs on the Mountain Limestone of Derbyshire*, Cade & Co, London, 1961

3. SOME IMPORTANT ARTICLES IN CLIMBING JOURNALS

ERNEST A. BAKER, 'Practice Scrambles in Derbyshire', *Climbers' Club Journal*, Vol 1, 1898

HENRY BISHOP, 'Climbs on Mountain Limestone in Derbyshire', *Climbers' Club Journal*, Vol 12, 1910

ALF BRIDGE, 'The Technique of Falling', *Mountaineering Journal*, June 1932

ERIC BYNE, 'My Unconquerables', *Midland Association of Mountaineers Journal*, 1951

—— 'What's in a name?', *Midland Association of Mountaineers Journal*, 1956

—— 'The Limestone Invasion', *Midland Association of Mountaineers Journal*, 1958

C. F. CAMERON, 'Wharncliffe Crags', *Climbers' Club Journal*, Vol 4, 1902

DAVE COOK, 'True Grit', *Mountain*, 26, March 1973

—— 'The Battle for Kinder Scout', *Mountain*, 32, February 1974

RICE K. EVANS, 'Some Recent Additions to the Stanage Climbs', *Rucksack Club Journal*, Vol 5, 1923

PETER HARDING, 'A Rock Climbing Apprenticeship', *Rucksack Club Journal*, Vol 14, 1961

PAUL NUNN, 'Derbyshire and Yorkshire Letter', *New Climbs*, The Climbers' Club, London, 1966

JIM PERRIN, 'Right Unconquerable', in *Hard Rock*, ed. Ken Wilson, Hart-Davis, MacGibbon, London, 1974

—— 'Playpower and The Cosmic Rascal', *Climber*, 1987

—— 'On the rock with Joe Brown', *Climber and Hillwalker*, 1990

A. S. PIGOTT, 'In Memoriam: Morley Wood', *Rucksack Club Journal*, 1934

HARRY SUMMERSGILL, 'In Memoriam: "Jeff"', *Rucksack Club Journal*, Vol 3, 1918

A profoundly moving obituary of Stanley Jeffcoat.

A. R. THOMSON, 'Ilam Rock', *Rucksack Club Journal*, Vol 3, 1915

Gripping.

MORLEY WOOD, 'Lesser Climbing', *Rucksack Club Journal*, Vol 5, 1924

As modest as the man himself. Full of interest.

ACKNOWLEDGEMENTS

This three-year project involved an enormous number of people, and simply to list them alphabetically would be to overrate the lesser contributions at the expense of those whose efforts were truly Herculean.

At the top of the list comes the 'home' climbing team who helped with many of the main climbing projects and were with me at many a 'production meeting' at a wide range of local alehouses: Steve Dean, biographer of Colin Kirkus, who gave me continual support throughout and supplied much useful research material; Chris Thorp, who also provided useful archaelogical papers; and Mike Pearce, who not only helped me setting up the ropes for some of the more alarming climbing shots, but excelled himself in creating the four very original maps in the book in exactly the way I wanted them, a gruelling task which involved many hours at the computer. A special mention must also be made of John Beatty, photographer and friend, for his generosity of spirit in sharing much of his vast knowledge of the Peak and, from his home in Bamford, giving me a virtually continuous update of weather conditions in the High Peak during the main photography of the book.

A wide range of people helped with specific photographic projects. In the order in which the images appear in the book: David Hope assisted with the night shoot of stars over Rainster, and Nick White, astrophotographer, gave very useful advice for shooting the Comet Hale-Bopp. For the monks riding past Nine Stones Circle, I was fortunate enough to secure the services of Jeremy Yeomans, who supplied and rode the historically authentic horses with fellow riders Kerry Saul and Mark Wolsey; Mr Swindell of Millfield Farm gave permission and was particularly helpful, Lynn Smith of Birmingham Costume Hire supplied the monks' habits, and Alan of Scanshop in Nottingham, using computer wizardry, increased the number of monks from three to eight. 'Daniel Defoe's trip to Chatsworth' involved a large number of people: Roger Wardle, Agent, and John Oliver, House Comptroller of Chatsworth gave me permission to use the track on Beeley Moor, Shirley Dalton and Caroline Dale-Leech of the Red House Stables Carriage Museum in Darley Dale supplied the carriage and pair, and Peter and his team drove it expertly. Bob McGovern, my next-door neighbour, bore an uncanny resemblance to Defoe, as portrayed in a contemporary engraving, once he was dressed in his wig (supplied by The Wig Centre, Nottingham), and Chris Thorp was 'the gentleman of his acquaintance'. The shot of the River Derwent below High Tor at Matlock was taken from a pontoon made of two canoes strapped together and skippered by Peter March of Derwent Training Services. For photographs from the Hunting Tower, Chatsworth Park, at different times of the year, the owner, Eddie Tennant, could not have been more helpful.

For the climbing photography in Chapter 8 I received an enormous amount of help. Most gratifying of all was obtaining the enthusiastic participation of some of the key names in British rock climbing, notably: John Allen, Joe Brown, Felicity Butler, Johnny Dawes, Seb Grieve, Peter Harding, Chris Jackson, Simon Nadin, and Richard McHardy (who also gave me much expert help and advice with the single rope techniques used in many of the climbing shots). Many other climbers went out of their way to help with specific projects, not all of which could eventually be used within the confines of this book: Malcolm Baxter (many projects), Mark Clark, Geoff Douglas ('Doug'), Ian Dunn ('Squawk'), Tom Gifford, Ruth Jenkins, John Lumb and Barbara, Dave Mawer, Kath Pyke, Matthew ('Joe') Rhodes, Pete Rowlands, Pete and Kate Sutton, Sam Whittaker, Bill Wintrip, and Mick Wrigley. Then there were all those who helped with such unglamorous tasks as holding ropes, belaying friends etc., or who were cajoled, on the crag, into performing for the camera: Jonathan Batty and Richard Crosby (who acted as 'stand-ins', or rather, laybackers, on Right Unconquerable to find the best camera angles a week before Joe Brown's visit), Dave Anderson from Salt Lake City, Keith Ashton, Paul Bannister, Joe Bawden, Stuart Brooks, John Cutcliffe, Pete George, Terry Gifford, David Heydecker, Leo Houlding, Pete Hulley, Tim James (one of my first climbing partners from the late sixties), Karl Key, Joe Lenham, Adam Long, Paul Mitchell, Shane Ohly, Adam Pepper, John Pereira, Pipps ('Le Chunks') Planques from France, Peter Roberts, Matt Saunders, Vicky Sherwood, Nick Taylor, Mark Tolver, Martin Veale, Tom Wash, Dave Whitley, and Mark Wilson.

For the history of rock climbing in the Peak many people made outstanding contributions. It was a particular joy to track down the pre-war pioneers, Frank Elliott and Arthur Birtwistle, both in good health and wonderful raconteurs, who provided me with a wealth of information. Also of great interest were: Frank Kiernan, now in his 90s and oldest surviving member of the Rucksack Club; Stanley Jeffcoat, son of the great Edwardian pioneer of the same name; Roy Bullen, friend of the late P A Barnes, conservationist and photographer of the twenties; Mona Schaanning, a distant relative of the Edwardian climbing photographer Alf Schaanning; and Albert Shutt, Dick Brown, John Loy, and Bob Dearman for their rivetting first ascent accounts. A large number of other people were also consulted, many at great length: Ruth Allen, wife of the late, great Nat Allen of the Valkyrie and Rock and Ice Clubs; John Llewellyn, the Rucksack Club archivist; Peter Bamfield; Geoff Birtles; Paul ('Tut') Braithwaite; Mike Browell; Joe Brown; Derrick Burgess; Derek Carnell; Don Chapman; Dennis Gray; Pete Greenwood; Dave Gregory; Peter Harding; Ken Herbert; Tony Howard; Geoff Milburn; Ben Moon; David Penlington; Ernie Phillips; Geoff Pigott (son of Fred Pigott); Harry Pretty; Tom Proctor; Reg Pullinger; Steve Read; Tony Riley; Ken Tarbuck; Ron Townsend; and Tom Waghorn. Ken Wilson was, as always, a most helpful fund of information whenever I consulted him. Margaret Ecclestone, Librarian of the Alpine Club, gave access to ancient climbing journals, and Malcolm Baxter, Steve Dean, John Lumb and Mark Clark lent valuable out-of-print books.

For original research into the general history of the Peak the main sources were: the Derbyshire Record Office, Matlock; the Local Studies Library, Derby; and several local historians: Trevor Brighton, Marion Alcroft of the Bradwell Historical Society, Hilary Clarke of Great Longstone, Geoff Lester of Winster, and Derek Wain of Whatstandwell. For help on the Robin Hood legend: the Duke of Rutland, and his secretary, Mrs D A Staveley; and on this and a range of other subjects, Roly Smith, editor of 'Peak and Pennine' magazine, and Apra Books of Sandiacre who miraculously obtained several out-of-print books for me at very short notice. For information on the Duke's and Robin Hood quarries at Whatstandwell, Ian Thomas of the Stone Centre, Wirksworth.

For permission to reproduce old paintings, prints and photographs: John Pickin, who supplied the original drawing of the Celtic headhunter; the Head Verger of Derby Cathedral for allowing me to photograph the Buck in the Park emblem by Robert Bakewell; Peter Day, the Chatsworth curator, and the Chatsworth Settlement Trustees, for permission to reproduce the painting of Elizabethan Chatsworth by Richard Wilson; the Librarian of the Derby Local Studies Library for the print of the execution of Jeremiah Brandreth; Mansfield Brewery for permission to use part of the pub sign of the Robin Hood Inn; Grant Jarvis of Jarvis Books for two archive photographs of early climbers in the Peak; Mark Goodwin for the extract from his poem 'Craft'; and Jim Perrin for a wide range of quotations from his writings. A very special mention must be made of Ernie Phillips, climber and photographer, who not only gave me a mass of historical information, but lent me his entire collection of photographs and original negatives, including the classic 1949 pictures of Joe Brown on the Unconquerables at Stanage.

Then there are those who helped in a variety of ways which do not fall easily into tidy categories: Fred Mellor of Great Longstone, Mary Wilson of Ashford in the Water, and John Wilson of Buxton, for the trail which led to Stanley Jeffcoat's son; Bill Brogden of Hopton Hall; Val Brown; Simon Seligman, the Chatsworth Publicity Officer; Martin Trafford for access to the Roaches Hut; Robert of the Barrel Inn, Bretton, for giving me an on-the-spot report of a temperature inversion; the Druid Inn, Birchover, who helped me find the riders for the monks-on-horseback shot; the Gamecock Inn and Dan Kilyan of Harbury in Leicestershire for helping me track down the artist John Pickin, now living in Scotland; and David and Carrie Jones, for general support and for providing me with a London base whenever it was needed.

For a whole range of technical matters and for the film processing I must thank Nick, Jason, and the rest of the team at Multiprint Laboratories in Derby; Max Hale of Fujifilm; Scanshop in Nottingham for Photoshop work on photographs on pages 52, 53, 54, 73, and 144; and Caving Supplies, Buxton, and Shaun Puckering of Hitch n Hike, Bamford, for specialist climbing equipment and advice.

Early drafts of the text were read by Steve Dean, Tim and Teresa James, and my parents, Peter and Dorothy, who all made very useful comments and suggestions. My father in particular gave valuable help on a number of historical points. Viv Stainforth suggested the title of the book which eventually came home to roost, and my brother John helped on various recces and some of the more difficult climbing shots.

Finally I must thank John Parker, my agent, and Carol O'Brien, the Editorial Director at Constable, for their support throughout; and Richard Tomkins, the Art Director at Constable, for his help on a host of technical and typographical matters.

As far as the overall production was concerned, the book was conceived, researched, written, photographed, designed, and typeset entirely by myself, using Pagemaker 6.5 on a Power Macintosh computer. The maps, by Mike Pearce, were created on Corel Draw 7 using a PC.

INDEX

Plates are shown by *italic* page numbers, plates and text by ***bold italics***